Contents

Introduction

Literacy and community:
developing a primary curriculum through partnerships

Literacy and community

This book starts with large ambitions. Getting to grips with big concepts like 'literacy' and 'community' may seem to be a tricky task. 'Literacy' itself is a slippery term: does it include more than reading and writing? Of course, because the basis for these must be speaking and listening. Does it involve more than books? Of course, because of the many different forms of text - on paper and on screen - that permeate our everyday lives. So literacy is about texts of all kinds and the ways in which children learn to read and understand them. But also and how they forge their literate identities through their preferences and experiences. And what about 'community'? Does that mean within the school or outside it? The district, or different groups of people living in the area, nation or world? And should it be 'community' or 'communities'? What is clear is that any definition of community should include a sense of shared values, even if there are differences, and some kind of social cohesion. Schools are in a key position to become the hub for social cohesion within the areas they serve - to bring home and school closer together and to develop shared aims for the children who inhabit both. Similarly, classrooms have the potential to encapsulate all the elements of harmonious diversity which are features of successful communities, to recognise what each member of the group can contribute and to build on that. However, there are often mis-matches between the ideal and the reality and sometimes a view that homes are deficient in the values that schools want to promote (Cremin *et al.*, 2011; Comber, 2007; Comber and Kamler, 2004).

Much work on the relationship between home and school has highlighted a need for greater two-way traffic between the two (Muschamp *et al.*, 2007; Marsh, 2003). Traditionally, schools have seen parents as the recipients of information about 'how we teach your children' or 'what we expect of you and your children', although there's nothing necessarily wrong with that. What is missing is a reciprocal question or two about what 'funds of knowledge' (Gonzalez *et. al.*, 2005) the children might bring to school, what kinds of social and cultural capital they draw on from their home and community experience. The research project *Building Communities: Researching Literacy Lives* concluded that:

> ...if children are not to experience a potentially debilitating gap between literacy and learning inside and outside school, then the profession needs to re-conceptualise literacy to build on children's everyday literacy experiences and funds of knowledge. (Cremin *et al.*, 2011: 4)

At the same time, the report called for schools and teachers to take a good look at their assumptions and perceptions about homes and families in order to create a more productive relationship between the two (see Table 1).

Expectations and the curriculum

According to Kress:

> *One of the major problems for young people in schools [is] the gap between the expectations that they bring from their world and the expectations that exist in the school from a former world.*
> (Kress, 2005: 294)

This book explores expectations: teachers' expectations of what young learners can and cannot do; children's expectations of what school might offer in relation to their identities outside the classroom; parents' expectations of how school will foster their children's abilities. And, of course, government's expectations of what ought to be going on in schools. The Expert Panel advising the government on the National Curriculum (DfE, 2011) sees a distinction between a school curriculum and a national one. Most particularly, the panel urges that schools should design a school curriculum that best meets the needs of their pupils in their localities:

> There are a number of components of a broad and balanced school curriculum that should be developed on the basis of local or school-level decision making, rather than prescribed national Programmes of Study. (DfE, 2011: 6)

The expectation here, then, is that schools should have the freedom to design and construct a curriculum for their own purposes that will best suit the school and wider community that they serve. But this freedom carries responsibility to consider just what the needs of the children and their families might be. New (in

Literacy and community: developing a primary curriculum through partnerships

1

College Lane, Hatfield, Herts. AL10 9AB
Information Hertfordshire
Services and Solutions for the University

For renewal of Standard and One Week Loans,.
please visit the web site http://www.voyager.herts.ac.uk

This item must be returned or the loan renewed by the due date.
A fine will be charged for the late return of items.

Contents

Schools and teachers with more school-centric perspectives and orientations tend to...	Schools and teachers with more open/less school-centric perspectives and orientations tend to...
Be framed by the standards performance-based agenda	Challenge the standards agenda and work to a set of broader outcomes
Measure literacy attainment through performance in standardised tests	See standard literacy tests as part of a wider set of literacy achievements and interests
Conceive of learning as school-based	Recognise that learning happens in multiple contexts in and out of school
Focus on school literacy	Focus on school and everyday literacies
Provide families with information about school literacy	Find out about children's everyday literacy practices and funds of knowledge
Legitimate what the system recognises alone	Value and legitimate students' out-of-school experience
Construct one-way traffic between school and home	Foster and value two-way traffic between home and school
Teach the National Curriculum	Tailor the National Curriculum in responsive ways and draw on children's funds of knowledge
Focus on teaching	Focus on teaching and learning
Retain professional distance and more hierarchical positions	Build close professional and more equivalent teacher-parent-child relationships

Table 1: A conceptualisation of school positioning in relation to parents and families (Cremin *et al.*, 2011: 3)

2012) Ofsted guidance emphasises the importance of 'promoting the engagement of parents and carers in their children's learning' (Ofsted, 2011: 20) and engaging the school community as a whole. In other words, schools and teachers are being urged to see the bigger picture of what a school curriculum can offer children's learning, and external and internal evaluation requires schools to consider how they provide for the diversity of the school population. This requires some confidence to be flexible and open to the opportunities offered by partnerships.

The contributors to *Literacy and community: developing a primary curriculum through partnerships* offer a view of that wider horizon, seeing, for example, that literacy means more than may be traditionally conceived and that children's community and cultural experience can be the starting point for building learning. The book is based on a commitment to a culturally inclusive approach to literacy teaching and learning which reflects the language(s) and cultures of the community and wider society and includes the experiences of pupils, parents and community members, seeing partnership as essential [1]. Covering a range of topics and presenting case studies of classroom, whole school and local authority projects, contributions are drawn from a range of school environments in metropolitan boroughs, suburban and rural settings, describing collaborations which see children, family members, carers, teachers and other members of the school community as partners in furthering children's achievements. Threading throughout the chapters is a belief that the individual child's knowledge and experience can be fruitfully harvested through a school curriculum which looks outward, valuing the contributions of families and local communities, as well as inward to the creation of a vigorous and thriving school community.

Notes

[1] With thanks to Jane Bednall and the Newham EMA team for sharing their framework for a culturally inclusive approach.

Chapter 1
Working with parents in the nursery
Sharon Fell

Context

The Ronald Openshaw Nursery Education Centre (RONEC) is situated in the north eastern corner of the London borough of Newham. Most families live in rented accommodation, many in short term lettings. It has been on its present site for over twenty years and has developed enormously to cater for changing needs and demands. It is a three class setting for 3-5 year olds (approximately 120 places) and has extended day care provision for 2-4 year olds. It has provision for children with profound and multiple learning difficulties and has welcomed exchange staff visits from Holland and Russia to share exemplary practice and expertise. A variety of services are offered to support parents e.g. parent, carer and toddler sessions and ESOL and ICT classes. The setting is culturally and linguistically diverse - the largest groups being Black African, Bangladeshi and Other White backgrounds (i.e. Eastern European and Travellers). Around 75% of children speak, or have access to, a language other than English. About half of all children are at the early stage of acquiring English when they start nursery. Approximately 36 languages are spoken by families.

> **The school engages parents and carers exceptionally well, which contributes greatly to outstanding community cohesion.** Ofsted, January 2011

At the time of this project I was Ethnic Minority Achievement advisory teacher for the London borough of Newham, working within the setting with EMA/Traveller team colleagues Nighat Yasmin and Anthea Wormington, EMA nursery nurse Meena Bhambra, parents and children to:

- encourage parents (especially from vulnerable/isolated) ethnic groups to share their experiences and wealth of expertise to broaden, enrich and make more relevant the learning experiences of their children and to make them feel welcomed and able to participate within the setting
- highlight the importance of language and communication (in home language) at home
- develop approaches to pre-literacy activities at home by sharing ideas for practical activities.

Three short case studies show different approaches to achieving these aims.

Case study one **Distant Lands - Travelling Voices**

For some years the Nursery Education Centre has carried out projects involving parents. In the autumn term of 2005 the Newham Ethnic Minority Achievement team were involved in a parental involvement project with Bangladeshi mothers, aiming to draw this particular community into the parent-based activities run in the setting. The project was very well received and parents asked for more, similar projects. In addition, for many years the staff at the setting have organised an annual summer carnival involving children, parents and the local community. The carnival theme for 2006 was Moving On - a Traveller's Tale. It celebrated stories about why people and animals have to travel to unfamiliar territory at certain times in their lives. Various projects were set up by the nursery to work on this theme, for example, the local Traveller community who were relocating to a different site, produced a film which was a lasting legacy to their residing in the area. These experiences suggested the potential for the project Distant Lands - Travelling Voices about how we all came to be living in Stratford, Newham.

I was invited to work with Meena Bhambra (EMA nursery nurse) and the parents' group, continuing to focus particularly on Bangaladeshi mothers. Meena already ran and organised many parent sessions and activities. We arranged a six session programme to:

- tell and record a personal story about coming to Newham
- visit a local place of interest - to raise confidence and encourage independent visits with family members
- design and produce a banner for the carnival.

During the sessions parents looked at examples of similar projects and photographs (primarily short, personal recounts from the website: www.movinghere.org.uk) and shared their stories of how and why they had travelled/moved to Newham. They then wrote their story, sometimes in home language, and these were typed up for publishing (Figure 1.1). They brought in photographs from home to illustrate their work and designed and made a front cover for their story (Figure 1.2). To support this work they visited the Museum of Immigration and Diversity in Princelet Street, Spitalfields, East London then they designed and made a banner for the carnival illustrating their stories. Finally they made a group book as a record of their work.

Sweet Dreams by Ferdous Ara

My name is Ferdous Ara Pasha. I am a Bangladeshi woman. I completed my education from Dhaka University. I got my graduation 2 masters in chemistry. Then I was married to Mr. Anwar Pasha who got his education from Dundee College of Textile Manchester UK, then returned to homeland and worked there.

He told me many stories, events sweet memories about this country. He wanted to visit this country along with me again, but unfortunately he expired leaving me alone in his early age when my three children, two daughters and one son was too small. Now his dreams come true. I am happy now my elder daughter got graduation and masters in Architect and my son is going to be a Tele communication engineer.

Again my another dream is that I am now in U.K. I came on 21st May 2006. I visited Manchester. I stayed there two days. In London I also visited Museum, History Museum, library, and this and that, many places but alone without my husband, but I have two sweet sweet grandsons with me. Thanks to Almighty for all.

It's wonderful to see your park specially which are very beautiful and well maintained. Other places are also nice, they should be as because it is a rich country you have money, education, knowledge. Another thing I am happy to see that you people are very nice and co-ordinating. The Muslims also do well here.

Figure 1.1 Ferdous Ara's story 'Sweet Dreams'

Figure 1.2 Cover of personal story

The stories told were moving, enlightening and positive. I doubt if we would have learnt so much about each other without this focus. As well as mothers, an aunt and grandmother also came to some of the sessions and Sham, a member of staff, was also eager to become involved with the project and wrote her story to go in the book. Seven stories were produced, showing a wide variety of experiences and how we all happened to be in Stratford. Some contributors were long term residents, one mother's husband was on a work contract and would be returning to Bangladesh the following year, another had come to meet her future husband and to marry, and a proud grandmother was on an extended visit to see her daughter and family.

The story writing and publishing allowed some mothers to develop new skills in a non-threatening environment, for example, not everybody had used a computer before. The trip to the Museum was a success and showed us how different groups of people had moved to East London, for a variety of reasons, in search of a better life, adding ingredients and experiences to this culturally vibrant and diverse hotpot - or jellied eels, dhal, rice and peas, moussaka… the suitable alternatives are endless!

Most parents were not able to come to every session. This was sometimes due to the timings of the session - Friday is not a convenient day for Muslim women, something that needed to be recognised and noted for the future. We had been aware of this but were unable to reschedule dates. Nevertheless they felt comfortable to drop in when they had time, and yet still everything came together - the banner and book were made and we went on the trip (Figure 1.3). Everybody gained something from the project and everyone was proud of what they had achieved.

Figure 1.3 Parents with the banner they designed and made with their children

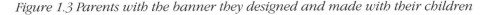

Case study two **Multimodal project: weather and climate change**

The setting was keen to link a project with their current topic and the carnival theme for 2010 which was 'Weather and Climate Change'. The aims of the project were to:

- develop speaking and listening, encouraging use of topic based vocabulary using photographs and real objects
- create weather-themed multimodal texts with children using digital photographs and a variety of props
- develop children's ICT skills and computer based mark making
- make a book of the photos to share with setting and parents.

Meena Bhambra, the nursery nurse from the Ethnic Minority Achievement team, was also involved in the organisation of the groupings and other activities. A room with an interactive whiteboard was made available with props and a laptop computer (Figure 1.4). On the first day the children worked in groups of two or three. They looked at and talked about a whiteboard slideshow of photographs in different weather conditions from around the world. They then chose one they wanted to work with. The children dressed themselves or a teddy, or both, using props that we had provided then took pictures of each other (Figure 1.5).

Above: Figure 1.4 Table of props

Left: Figure 1.5 Dressing for the photographs

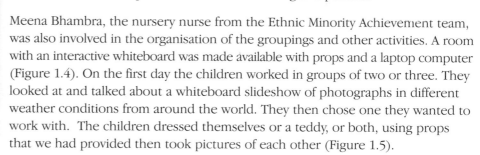

We encouraged the children to talk about what they were doing, the choices they were making and why. Before the next session I loaded the children's chosen weather photographs on to the computer ready for use in a PowerPoint™ programme the following day. The photographs of themselves were also printed off so that children could remember what they had been doing, how they were dressed and to choose which one they wished to stick on their weather picture.

The next day, working in the same groups, the children added comments to their photographs in speech bubbles and banners. Many tried mark making in the speech bubbles using Word Art to choose how they wanted to write their name. Twins Siana and Rositsa were helped by their grandmother who was attending ESOL classes. They talked to her about the pictures in Bulgarian and she translated some words into Bulgarian for me. Their grandmother enjoyed seeing the activity and working with the girls. This again was an activity that all children were able to participate in, including children who were naturally quiet, and children with special or physical needs.

Twenty three children were involved in the project. Meena knew which children who would work comfortably together and grouped the children accordingly. Many benefited from seeing good peer modelling of language. It gave children the opportunity to make choices about what picture/type of weather/props they wanted to use. They were able to discuss and give reasons for their choices. They could talk about what familiar to them, for example, recognising the photographs of the outside environment of the setting, remembering building a snowman in the snow or visiting the seaside. Children were encouraged to stay in the role play area looking at photographs but were able to ask when they wished to return to class. However, many remained focused for the whole period they were in the room, on average thirty minutes.

These activities provided a very good context for observations and assessment, particularly in speaking and listening, the children's knowledge about weather and their use of appropriate vocabulary. It gave Meena and other support staff an opportunity to observe children and pass on observations to key workers. The children enjoyed looking at photographs of themselves on the computer and talking about the photos. Many enjoyed mark-making and exploring the keyboard and it was an activity that interested both boys and girls. All children involved were able to participate at their own level, for example, some observing others or participating without speaking unless prompted while others took a lead role. Some children liked dressing up the teddies, others enjoyed dressing up themselves and some enjoyed doing both. Children with special needs/health issues were able to participate, contribute to and enjoy the activity.

The finished book was shared with parents and placed in the reception area of the setting, and copies of the children's finished work were put in their special work books (Figures 1.6 and 1.7).

Figure 1.6 Finished books

Case study three **Re-vamping the toy library**

The setting had identified a link between the rise in children's levels of attainment and parents attending ESOL classes. The parent, carer and toddler group was also proving increasingly popular with certain groups of parents and with a large increase in the number of children from Eastern Europe but Traveller families still remained a little on the periphery of the setting, it was felt another project was needed.

Meena had been running a successful toy library for a long time, but keeping tabs on different packs and mending and replacing lost or broken items was - and is - incredibly time consuming. She wanted to make even better use of the existing toy library: sorting, replenishing, mending, adding new activities and cataloguing and re-labelling items, making it more attractive to parents, easier to run and therefore more accessible. She wanted to encourage continued parental involvement in children's work, targeting particular groups, for example Traveller families. She also knew that working with parents was a good way to model and demonstrate activities, games and strategies which encouraged speaking, listening and cognitive development.

Figure 1.7 Collage of the children's pictures

The programme of sessions included a trip to the Bethnal Green Museum of Childhood to link with the theme of toys and festivals because past evaluations showed that many parents enjoyed trips (Figure 1.8). During the first sessions in the setting we played simple lotto, matching and dice games with parents and their children. Through these informal activities it soon became apparent that board and card games like snap were very popular with the Traveller families - both with adults and children. They were used to playing such games and liked learning new ones. We then moved on to making games to add to the toy library (Figure 1.9). These games could be taken home and played. After this parents sorted the toy packs and took photographs of the contents to laminate and attach to bags so that it was easy to see what the bags contained. After four sessions the library was completed and parents were keen to borrow the games they'd been playing.

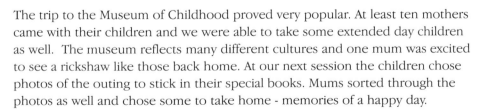

The trip to the Museum of Childhood proved very popular. At least ten mothers came with their children and we were able to take some extended day children as well. The museum reflects many different cultures and one mum was excited to see a rickshaw like those back home. At our next session the children chose photos of the outing to stick in their special books. Mums sorted through the photos as well and chose some to take home - memories of a happy day.

Figure 1.8 The trip to the Museum of Childhood

Left: Figure 1.9 Making the games

Two weeks later I revisited the setting to join the parent, carer toddler group. As requested by the parents, Meena and her colleague Kate were organising a cooking morning - making pizza. As usual, younger siblings were made welcome. Food is the universal topic. We all know something about it and it makes a wonderful talking point. During the morning I lost count of the different methods and ingredients used to make pizza. Everyone was slightly different, but all ideas were listened to and valued. The conversation digressed to hummus, and aubergine dip recipes were exchanged. Eventually the finished product was tried, tested, consumed and judged (Figure 1.10). Suggestions were put forward on how to improve next time.

Below: Figure 1.10 Making pizza

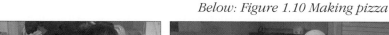

Conclusion

The parental links continue to be strong and well supported, so on reflection how successful is the setting in having an inclusive approach to literacy? And if so what makes them successful, bearing in mind that many of the children are in a pre-reading stage? Home language and literacy is valued and encouraged. The ethos of the setting encourages everyone to feel valued and able to be themselves. This was evident in case study one where the wonderful use of language by the parents - poetic, sharing personal feelings and experiences - illustrated their trust in sharing their stories. The response from parents is always very positive, with many wishing to attend sessions and wanting to do activities with their children. They found working with their children interesting and enlightening. It enabled them not only to interact with them in an activity but also to observe how their child interacted with other adults and peers. But perhaps the most important aspects were that staff and parents could work together, learning from each other and listening to each other, broadening everybody's knowledge and understanding.

Acknowledgements

Grateful thanks to staff, parents and children at The Ronald Openshaw Nursery Education Centre who have been such an inspiration and fun to work with.

Reflections

• How do you encourage parents to work alongside their children in your setting/classroom?
• What is the impact of this kind of work on the children's achievements?
• How do you draw on and value home language and literacy in your setting/classroom?

Working multimodally:
taking bilingual pupils beyond the literal
Jane Bednall and Pavanbir Sarkaria

Jane Bednall, Ethnic Minority Adviser (EMA) and Pavanbir Sarkaria from Elmhurst school, team-taught, evaluated and developed a year 3 cross curricular project as part of a CPD partnership between the EMA team and Newham schools. In the London borough of Newham there are at least 127 languages spoken in school communities and in the year 3 class involved in the project the majority of children were of Muslim or Hindu faiths.

In order to develop the children's language skills, reading and writing, at Elmhurst the senior management team and teachers have developed and embedded multimodal, culturally inclusive projects or units of work in every year group. In this way the school is developing a 'mainstream model' of working with bilingual children, using and refining inclusive practices that raise achievements in oral and written language. It is a positive model of bilingual children rather than a model that marginalises these pupils by withdrawal. The school feels it is important to recognise the children's developing bilingualism as a positive force not an 'EAL problem' so often described (Anderson and Chung, 2009).

Scaffolding for challenge in learning

All children, but perhaps particularly bilingual children, need learning that challenges their thinking and develops their academic language (Garcia, 2009). This challenge needs to be made accessible and scaffolded by inclusive teaching and learning approaches. The Planning Access Key devised by the Newham EMA team is based on researched strategies that make learning accessible for bilingual pupils but are inclusive for all children.

The Planning Access Key for Ethnic Minority Learners

In order for all pupils to reach common outcomes the following strategies need to be embedded in planning:

1. High quality, culturally relevant materials
2. Peer support through mixed ability grouping
3. Collaborative learning in pairs/groups (e.g. talk partners, investigative tasks)
4. Speaking and listening integral to activities
5. Vocabulary/word/phrase banks developed with pupils
6. Teacher/peer modelling of tasks and outcomes
7. Repetitive process and/or language
8. Opportunities to use first language/home language
9. Visual support
10. Real objects: props, puppets etc.
11. Graphic organisers (e.g. tables and bar charts)
12. Scaffolding for reading tasks
13. Scaffolding for writing tasks (e.g. writing frames)
14. Drama and role play
15. Interactive, multilingual displays
16. Clearly identified roles for adults
17. Opportunity for all pupils to have a voice
18. Opportunity for all pupils to show understanding and learning
19. Parental involvement
20. Homework that is supportive of the classroom curriculum.

Creativity and cultural context

This project illustrated how creative multimodal ways of working can raise achievement in reading and writing for bilingual pupils. As Anderson and Chung argue, the 'perceived shortcomings' of traditional approaches to second language learning illustrate the importance of 'renewed interest in using creative works such as stories and drama to engage bilingual learners and provide an appropriate level of cognitive challenge' (Anderson and Chung, 2009: 16-17). However, although the focus of this chapter is on the achievement of bilingual pupils, all pupils benefit from these ways of working.

The project was developed around the work of the Bangladeshi poet Jasimuddin and his saga love poem 'Naskhi-Kanthar Math' - 'The Field of the Embroidered Quilt'. This text was related to the quilts made by Bangladeshi women to represent stories (Figure 2.1).

Figure 2.1 A quilt of the embroidered cloth made by Bangladeshi women

The aim of the unit of work was to make a multimodal scroll - a saga poem with words and images. Each child in the mixed ability year 3 class was to write a verse as part of a class poem and make an accompanying painted or pastel image. The children would work in pairs to read the images and verses of the poem. The whole class would take responsibility for decisions about the layout and design of the final scroll.

Using Jasimuddin's saga poem and images from quilts meant that children could move between images and words to explore the lyrical language and meanings of this rich, complex and challenging poem. Nighat Jasmin from the Newham EMA team brought the Bengali text, a beautifully English translated version of the poem and an embroidered cloth from Bangladesh.

Biographical details of Jasimuddin

Jasimuddin (1903-1976) is one of the most significant poets of Bangladesh. In Bengali literature Jasimuddin is known as 'Palli Kabi', a rural poet. Bangladesh is an agriculturally-based country and although industrialisation is now taking place, the majority of the people live in villages and their lives are in one way or another related to agriculture. The main subject of Jasimuddin's poetry was the lives of the people of rural Bengal. His deep involvement in communal socio-political movements, championing the cause of Bengali language and literature gives his lyric and folk poetry a sense of commitment and protest. His poems are popular as part of the school curriculum in West Bengal, India and Bangladesh.

'The Field of the Embroidered Quilt' is the story of two young people, Rupa and Shaju. They live in two adjacent villages. One day Rupa goes to collect bamboo and sees Shaju by the river that runs between the villages. They fall in love. They eventually marry after vividly described wedding preparations. Then one day Rupa is involved in a serious fight defending his village against rice thieves. He is unjustly arrested, taken to jail and never returns to his wife. Shaju loved her husband very dearly; she pines for him and becomes ill. She decides to make a quilt as a tribute to the love for her husband. Shortly after completing the quilt she dies. She had previously asked her mother to hang the quilt on a bamboo near her grave. Rupa is released from prison and when he sees the quilt near Shaju's grave, after playing the flute, he dies of grief.

Key aspects of teaching and learning

In all the projects developed in Newham we have found that visual literacy, critical literacy, enquiry based learning and emotional literacy are keys to effective teaching and learning. If these are regularly planned for they facilitate children's reading and writing skills. The first week's lessons were focused on developing the children's visual literacy and role play to develop their reading skills. The emphasis was on the importance of the children giving varied answers and their own viewpoints when reading the poem and texts, and asking questions of them. Once this openness is established, more children participate orally in the classroom because they know their different opinions are valued.

We began by using a Bengali story scroll, the Gazi scroll (from the British Museum website). This is one of many very long visual story scrolls which would be a central part of a multimodal performance narrative, hung from tall trees or along a path while singers, dancers and narrators perform the story around the scroll. The Gazi scroll tells a story in pictures of life in the Ganges delta and shows people of the Hindu faith living their lives and praying in temples. It also represents a Muslim 'saint' travelling through this area to spread the faith of Islam We also used *Tsunami* (Chitrakar, 2009), a contemporary poem in the style of a Bengali story scroll and a book about the Singh sisters' paintings (Quilly and Sekules, 2005). These quality models supported the children's writing, image making, design and layout. We believed that these texts would have cultural relevance and resonance for parents and children in the school community.

We hoped that building partnerships with homes would increase the children's motivation, support the curriculum and encourage dialogue at home about the children's learning. We sent letters to families explaining the project and asking them to talk to their children about any stories they knew related to the texts we were using. The children took home colour copies of the Gazi scroll and the quilt pictures to read with their parents. Although not many children re-told stories to the whole class that their parents had told them from talking about the Gazi scroll, it became evident that the children and parents were talking about the project at home. For example, Shanjida's parents supported her to summarise Jasimuddin's poem in Bengali so she could tell this to the class.

The culturally inclusive texts were chosen to encourage children to relate their own life and faith experiences to their learning. When learning about Bangladesh as background to Jasimuddin's poem many children were able to tell stories about family visits there. The experiences of other children meant that they could discuss similarities and differences between rural Pakistan and Bangladesh. These family experiences helped them to understand the setting of the poem and unpick the differences of rural life and their urban life in London.

Important as it is to use culturally inclusive texts, it is equally important that these texts model the highest quality language and image. Jasimuddin uses language that is lyrical, figurative and powerfully challenging. The poem paints with words just as we wanted to enable the children to do. The combination of words and images allows children to go beyond the literal - the words alone - to become creative and critical readers. To encourage the children to recognise and use their own diverse language skills, we read Jasimuddin's poem in Bengali and English.

Although the texts we used were particularly pertinent to the children in this particular school, the processes used in the project would be relevant in any classroom. Pupils should recognise themselves in the texts, resources and strategies used across the year and although it may not be possible to represent every pupil's heritage or choice of popular culture in every lesson, over a year it is possible to use a number that they are familiar with. Equally it is important that as global citizens we should all learn and be enriched by the diversity of cultures in our world. For example, we would consider it appropriate for children from a Cumbrian farming community to work interculturally and to study Jasimuddin's poem perhaps in comparison to poems from the British Isles describing rural life. In this example, the Cumbrian children would bring a depth of knowledge to the poems drawn from their own experience.

Working multimodally with gesture, image and words enabled the seven year olds to understand the complex poem and to develop their thinking skills. The Framework for Critical Analysis (Figure 2.2) brings together for children the development of their visual literacy skills, questioning skills and critical literacy skills. In order to encourage the children to ask questions of the visual texts they were reading, they noted their queries and observations. These would be used later in their poetry. The Framework acts as a scaffold to enable pupils to explore the context and layers of meaning of the story before they hear and read the complex language of the written text (Figure 2.3).

Framework for Critical Analysis

What do you know already?

What questions do you want to ask about the picture? Think of these questions:

Who?	**Why?**

Photocopy of an image or double page spread from a book

Where?	**How?**

What?

Figure 2.2 Framework for Critical Analysis

Framework for Critical Analysis

What do you know already? I know that they are feeling happy together because of there exsppresions.

15

What questions do you want to ask about the picture? Think of these questions:

Who? This is Rupa and Shaju and they are getting married

Why? Why are they holding a long stick with a leaf on it between them.

Where? This is Rupa and Shaju in a small village and it looks like a lovely beatifull wedding hall.

How? How did they decorate their cloths and decorations so beautifully?

What? What are the love birds saying to each other and what are they thinking of each others cloths?

Figure 2.3 Imaan's Framework for Critical Analysis

Scaffolding can also be provided by texts themselves. For part of the project Nighat Yasmin and I read aloud in Bengali and English a section of the poem which describes Rupa and celebrates the rural farmer. The language is complex, lyrical and moving:

> *Black is the pupil of my eye*
> *Black the ink with which I write*
> *Black is Birth and Death is Black,*
> *Black the universal Night.*
> *Black is the Son of the Soil and yet*
> *Victor is he of all*
> *He who with gold createth gold*
> *Has credit small.*
> *Only give me the colours, Brother,*
> *And I, even I,*
> *Can make the garland of the rainbow,*
> *Span the stormy sky.*

The class poems

Two class poems were made, starting with one of the children's questions generated when they looked at the quilt: 'Where is this village?' They understood that the use of questions throughout their poem has the effect of 'hooking' the reader in.

One of the class poems - *Rupa and Shanju*

Where is this peaceful village?
The birds are singing sweetly and calmly.
The grass is swinging side to side,
It's like people dancing in the wind.
The villages are talking loudly.
Everything is just pretty
It's like an image of heaven.

   Shanjida

Down in the village the water goes to Rupa's
   lovely village.
The plants dance like the women dance to bring
   the great monsoon,
To grow the rice plants.
They rush in their houses made of bamboo
To keep the people cosy from the great monsoon.

   Uzair

The village
The big bamboos
The birds finally flying
Parrots are singing beautifully
People are dancing wildly
Flowers are dancing slowly
People are cooking, spicey smells
Rice in the air.

   Faizan

Who is this boy…?
Who is this boy with the long curly hair?
Rupa shiney as a red car.
Flowers scented of perfume.
Patterned trousers
With red colours

   Majedul

By looking in each others eyes.
They love the sight.
As Shanju looked at Rupa's long, black
   shiny hair.
She thought I want to marry him.
Then Rupa thought I want to marry her.
Have a beautiful wife and kids.
They were two young birds looking
For the beauty in each other.
They were both two lovers.
In the wedding hall they looked into each
   other's soul.
He is my lover and forever.
Sorrow's coming, do they know ?
I don't know
I don't think.

   Imaan

Birds are flying. Rupa I love you.
Where are you ?
I need you in my life.
Come back to my life.
Please.
Shaju wear all those beautiful saris and those
  pretty bangles
I love you
So much kisses and hugs from me.

  Shanjida

By looking at each other's eyes
They loved the sight.
As Shanju looked at Rupa's long black
  shiny hair.
She thought I want to marry him
Then Rupa thought I want to marry her.
They had a beautiful life.
They are birds flying slowly in the beautiful
  shiny sky.
There is a pretty house next to the long river.
They are mysterious green leaves.
There are small beautiful leaves.
Rupa found lots of bamboos in the forest and
Shanju found a bit of water.

  Zaibaida

Singing and dancing all day long.
The colourful bangles put on her delicate arms.
The sound of the vibrant bangles echoing and
  filling the room.
The fragrance of Rupa's love can be smelt on
  Shanju.
The rich colour of Mehndi, shows how deep
  their love is for each other.
The beads on my sari show that I love u!
Please take my hand in yours.

  Zareena

Busting time
Down to Rupa's fight, he got into a fight.
They were fighting with sticks.
Then when the policemen came,
The wife was crying because Rupa's got to go
to jail.
Then Rupa said, 'I will come back sometime.'
The trousers of Rupa was stitched and red
and
  patterned.
Then Rupa was struggling and said, 'don't
take me.'
Then Shaju may stay alive.
The birds were making noise.

  Kishan

Hopes and dreams shattered.
As two lovers are torn apart.
Down at the fight were people strike.
Leave it up to the policemen who ruin peo-
ple's lives.
This might be the end of Shaju's life.
But Shaju can't let that happen tonight.
Rupa and Shaju will die one night.
But there will stay forever even on daylight.

  Amaan

When I first met Rupa
My heart was full of love.
Now he is gone. I am now heart broken.
I have written this because it's now the end.

  Uzair

A cloth stitched of love
Will he come back to me?
Rupa is my heart and my soul.
I will never forget him.
He is like the village birds singing,
The beautiful butterflies flying.
Everything is filled with
Your memories.
I am filled with sadness and sorrow.

  Maisha

18

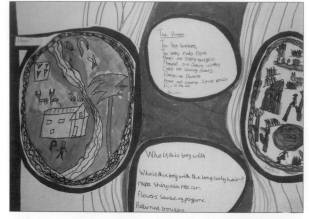

Figure 2.4 The village: introductory verses and images of the class poem

In his verses (Figure 2.4), Majedul describes the main male character Rupa, and starts with a question again: 'Who is this boy with the long curly hair?'

He creates a later line: 'patterned trousers with red colours' from his observation of Rupa's image on the quilt. This continual working between word and image shows how the children draw on both as they come to understand how to use figurative language.

Figure 2.5 Children's images of wedding preparation and marriage

From the poem as a whole it is clear how a multimodal approach supported the children's growing ability to use the poetic language of complex metaphor and carefully chosen descriptive terms. The class had explored the characters' actions and feelings through drama, reading the gestures of the poem's characters from the quilt images. They had worked on their own images of the poem so that they sought figurative language to create images for the readers of their poem. Uzair describes movement with: 'The plants dance like the women dance to bring the great monsoon' and Imaan captures the deep emotion felt by the lovers: 'They were two young birds looking/ For the beauty in each other.

The children were able to draw on their families' experience of weddings and preparation for them (Figure 2.5). The teacher brought in slides of her cousin's wedding, and they talked about mehndi patterns and included references in the poem: 'The rich colour of mehndi, shows how deep their love is for each other.

Figure 2.6 'A cloth stitched of love' Maisha's image of Shaju making the quilt

'Like pebbles in a river'

The children had made their images for the scroll whilst also drafting and re-drafting their verses. This meant they could work between word and image in their text making as they had done in their reading - creating layers of meaning. In Maisha's Chaucerian-like line 'A cloth stitched of love' (Figure 2.6) she illustrates her understanding of the symbolism of the quilt and Shaju's feelings. She uses a sophisticated image with use of perspective and also represents the Tree of Life echoing the simile in her verse:

'He is like the village birds singing
The beautiful butterflies flying.'

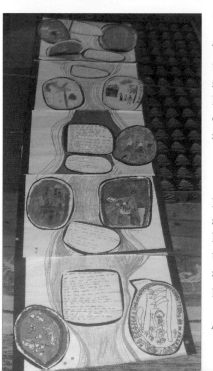

In the final session the children laid out their poems placing verses and images from sections in an agreed sequence. Two scrolls were made. As the class started to make their large scroll, one child suggested that the poem should be placed on a river, the river that ran between the two villages in the poem, showing remarkable insight into the symbolism of the river as a divisive element in relation to the love story. As the children placed their images in another said they were like 'pebbles in a river' (Figure 2.7).

Figure 2.7 One class scroll

Funds of knowledge: reflections on learning

In supporting bilingual children to develop sophisticated reading and writing skills it is important to make opportunities for them to have their voices heard. Realising that they have valuable funds of knowledge (Moll, 1992) drawn from their out of school experiences, we interviewed children to see if they could describe *how* they had learnt, including working multimodally and interculturally. We also asked pupils to analyse each other's work, hoping to build on the children's cultural capital (Bourdieu, 1986) (Figure 2.8).

1. What was your favourite part of the project? Why?

2. Which 3 activities did you enjoy the most? Write a sentence to explain why you liked them the most. (The different activities were: talking to your parents/carers about the pictures from quilt; hearing the poem in Bengali and in English; reading the poem by Jasimuddin; talking about the poem and asking questions about the poem; talking and asking questions about pictures from the quilt; drama and role play; writing your verse for the class poem; drawing and painting pictures for the class scroll; deciding how to lay out the scroll.)

3. What activities helped you learn and why?

4. Which activities (look at the list above) most helped you write your poem and make your picture?

5. What piece of work are you most proud of? Why?

6. Which part of your verse did you like the most and why?

7. Which part of your partner's verse did you like most and why?

8. Is there anything else you would like to have done during the project?

Figure 2.8 Questions about learning

What becomes evident is that children can articulate how working multimodally and how the choice of multimodal, culturally diverse and bilingual texts supported their learning. The children's appreciation of each other's work, and their own, showed that they had understood how the writer writes for the reader and how the writer uses poetic conventions to do that. When Imaan reads Maisha's verse she describes how the line 'A cloth stitched of love' tells the reader powerfully that the quilt 'was made for someone special'.

Imaan says the part of her own verse she finds the most powerful is:

In the wedding hall they looked into each other's soul,
Sorrow's coming, do they know?
I don't know
I don't think.

She describes how she wanted there to be 'a happy part then give a hint that bad things are going to happen because I want the reader to want to read more'. She understands that foreshadowing events can hold the reader's attention and has been inspired by Jasimuddin's saga poem with its mix of love, lyricism and tragedy. Maisha says she likes it that Imaan's reader 'doesn't know for sure' what will happen. A seven year old who understands the effect of creating uncertainty for the reader by using rhetorical questions, is a pupil who is a reader and writer working way beyond what might usually be expected for their age.

Shanjida described how using pictures related to the poem and other processes:

...[it] gave me lots of ideas and I understood the action and it made the class make lots of beautiful poems which I liked. Even I liked the drama because when other people was doing some drama it made me get some interesting ideas.

Humayra commented:

> *My favourite things that helped me learn were role-play, paintings pictures, writing poetry, when Nighat read in Bengali and was only using a little bit of English. The comics helped me with the poetry and the pattern on the carpet helped me with the pictures.*

Ali describes how he found the bilingual readings helped his comprehension:

> *Reading Jasimuddin's poem helped me when Nighat read it in English and in Bengali and Shanjida* [pupil who told the story of the poem in Bengali] *helped me.*

Faizan enjoyed the sound and action:

> *Working with a partner helped me, drama helped because it explains the action. Most of all hearing Jasimuddin's poem in Bengali because it sounded beautiful.*

Mushrat made list of all the things that had supported his learning:

> *1. The pictures and drama helped me get the ideas*
> *2. Using our imagination*
> *3. The action and the drama*
> *4. Looking at comics*
> *5. Looking at pictures of quality*
> *6. Rhyming in poems and in comics*
> *7. Reading the pictures of the Gazi scroll*

Maisha, an advanced bilingual learner, described her pleasure in making multimodal texts and how this affects the reader:

> *I loved the part when we all made a picture that we painted to connect with the poem. I learnt that people understand the story by reading our paintings and poems.*

She understood how diverse texts are inspirational models and certain texts supported different aspects of her learning:

> *The poem of Rupa and Shaju was very helpful to learn to write a poem, the comic books helped us tell 'stories' and the Bengali scroll mostly came in handy and helped us because we were going to make a scroll as well. The sand paintings (of Indian women of Milithia) gave us ideas for the writing and gave us clues for our pictures too.*

She also indicated that the various texts with images would support a pupil at the early stages of learning English:

> *Someone who does not know English might see the pictures and know what to do.*

and her pride in her work:

> *My favourite thing is the whole project, when we put our poems and pictures together when we did the scroll together that's why I'm so proud of me and the class. I discussed the project with my mum and dad they got interested and was very proud of me.*

Zaibaida saw the importance of hearing the mother tongue to support their learning:

> *When Shanjida told the story of the poem in Bengali I understood it.*

Many, boys particularly, commented on how role play and drama scaffolded their learning (Figure 2.9).

Figure 2.9 Communicating through gesture and expression

Majedul:

I think the role play helped me, the one when Rupa chopped the bamboo sticks and met Shaju because I knew what to write in my poem and the picture with his patterned trousers.

Nearat:

The drama helped me when we looked at the Gazi scroll when we saw characters good and bad.

Hawa appreciated the scaffolding:

I found the How, What, When work around the pictures about the poem helped me to think.

Reflections on the poems

The pupils' comments reveal their enjoyment in learning but also how they felt as readers of their work:

I'm most proud of the writing part because I've never wrote a poem before and I drew the fight because it was fun but I was not happy with the arresting part because Rupa did not do anything wrong.
Amaan

I am proud of my writing because I improved it in five afternoons. I enjoyed the poetry because I got excited.
Gintaras

I like our paintings because it looked like the Bengali story scroll and when I look at the drawings and the poem, it makes me think I am in there.
Nesrat

The children's comments also reflect their response to one of the key themes of the poem: understanding of the injustice of Rupa's wrongful imprisonment. Amaan asked:

'What's the point of arresting him when it wasn't his fault?'

He carries this theme through into his verse:

Hopes and dreams shattered as lovers are torn apart…
Leave it up to the policeman who ruins people's lives.

Suggested improvements to the project

Finally we interviewed children about the improvements they would make to the project. Kishan had a vision to make the poem scroll part of a more multimodal performance that would reflect its heritage and original use: 'I would like to put in dancing and sounds.'

Zaibaida took her authorship seriously and wanted a wider publication: 'I would have wanted to make a book or song because if people bought the book they would know the story well.'

Gintaras had recently arrived from Lithuania and found writing in English a struggle. Before the project he did not enjoy writing. When he evaluated the project he said he would find: 'Even more writing, more painting and even more exciting words' helpful. He was motivated by the scaffolding of the challenge, particularly the Framework, as well as the creativity of the approach. He was inspired by his work being part of a bigger whole, a vibrant unfolding scroll. He has now begun to write very confidently in all his lessons, finding the scaffold of building vocabulary, questions and ideas around images helpful as can be seen from the work he produced after the project on the lives of refugees and understanding how they feel (Figure 2.10).

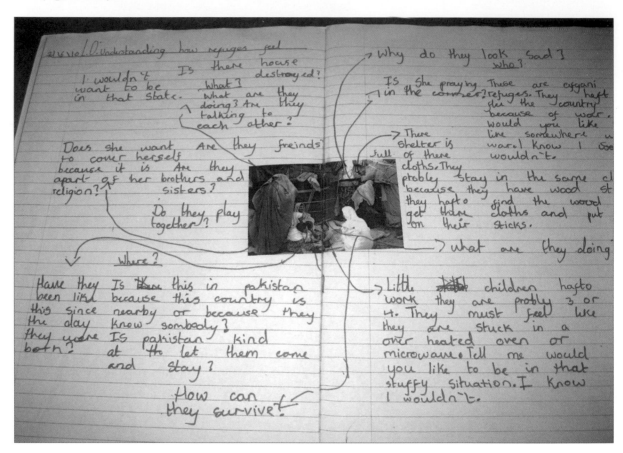

Figure 2.10 Gintaras's work 'Understanding how refugees feel'

Conclusion

The project was based on the view that it is essential that bilingual pupils - or any pupil - can read layers of meaning, develop their language beyond the literal, orally and in writing. The project demonstrated how using quality culturally relevant texts, including those in community languages, challenged and inspired the children to draw on their cultural expertise, to develop their language and raise their achievement in writing. Children as young as seven were working at a level of complexity, drawing on sophisticated poetic techniques in a way that would not be expected of children their age. The children's creativity was sparked by the challenge of the work and their achievements were scaffolded by working multimodally through gesture, image and word. In reflecting on their poems the children felt that working with bilingual texts had supported their learning. They were certainly able to evaluate their own work and each other's achievements with sophistication and feel real pride in their achievements. It was clear to us that making opportunities for children to voice their opinions and ideas - and then listening to and hearing their mature comments - allowed us to learn just how these ways of working motivate them and enable them to achieve highly.

Notes

[1] A version of this chapter was published in *English 4-11* (English Association and United Kingdom Literacy Association) Spring and Summer editions, 2012.

Acknowledgements

Thanks to Leanne Cranston's inspiration in establishing multimodal ways of working in Elmhurst primary school, Newham and the support given by Sukwinder Samra, deputy headteacher. Nighat Yasmin (from the Newham EMA team) also gave considerable support and advice.

Thanks also for use of the quilt image to:
www.sos-arsenic.net/lovingbengal/jasimuddin.html and
www.sos-arsenic.net/lovingbengal/quilt.html

Books used in the project

Worlds A-Part: Paintings by the Singh Twins (2005) Quilley, G., Sekules, V., Singh, R.K. and Singh A.K. UK: Twin Studio.

Reflections

- How might you use the principles of the Planning Access Key (page 11) to impact on teaching and learning in your classroom/school?
- How do you draw upon a range of texts from different cultures as part of your curriculum?
- How do you make opportunities for children to reflect on and evaluate their literacy learning?

UKLA

Building understanding, sharing identities: 'this is them to a tee!'

Rebecca Kennedy

Context

Yardley Wood community primary school is a one form entry school of 220 children in the south of Birmingham. The number of children eligible for free school meals (FSM) is more than three times the national average with the proportion of children with English as an additional language close to national average. Raising standards in literacy, particularly writing and development of the curriculum are a central part of the school development plan and the school has recently come out of an Ofsted category. School leaders are working to establish the school at the heart of its local community and there are new opportunities for family learning.

As part of a local authority curriculum development network, the senior leadership team had identified the following aims for curriculum design:

- to develop enthusiasm for learning and motivation to learn
- to provide an exciting curriculum linked to the community
- to raise standards in literacy.

This project was designed to explore children's identity with the hope of engaging family members to participate in the children's learning. They also wanted to develop a more cohesive curriculum by expanding opportunities to write in different subject areas.

Starting points

Katie Palmer is curriculum development leader and the year 5 teacher. For this project she worked alongside Rebecca Kennedy, a consultant, to develop a three week teaching sequence focusing on finding practical ways of implementing the school's aims for curriculum design. They wanted to develop opportunities to write across subjects and investigate curriculum planning with consideration to time, place, people and pedagogies. They also wanted to enthuse reluctant writers. The purpose of the teaching sequence was to explore what is meant by identity with an emphasis on citizenship, literacy and creativity. The unit outcome was a non-chronological report: All about me.

'I can very much see what kind of person they are.'

Katie began the unit of work by sharing several images of a famous personality. The class considered how he differed in the photographs, and the assumptions they made about his identity in different contexts. She explained that the children would be investigating how their own identities were shaped by the different circumstances of their lives - exploring their family history, their relationships with others and their connections to the community. They would investigate how these contributed to their sense of self, help shape their personalities and impact on how they perceive themselves.

Teacher and children bought in photographs of themselves from home. Katie knew that in order to gain children's confidence she needed to trust them with information about her own family. All photographs were shared, promoting genuine interest and informative talk; children recounted the time when images were taken and explained aspects of their lives. Following this, the children considered descriptions for their images and wrote kennings reflecting their thoughts.

Diandra	Jessica
Baby holder	*Fit netballer*
Dummy sucker	*Oldest classmate*
The sensible one	*Kind supporter*
Outside adventure	*Hard worker*
Smiling one	*Fast writer*

The kennings demonstrated that the children were considering the different roles they inhabit. Diandra's kenning 'The sensible one' refers to a photograph of her with her siblings. Jessica considered different attributes that she feels she has: 'Hard worker, fast writer, kind supporter'. Responses were personal, linked to the photographs they had selected to share with the class.

Photographic artwork created by Birmingham born artist, Gillian Wearing for her series, '*Signs that Say What You Want Them To Say and Not Signs that Say What Someone Else Wants You To Say*' 1992-3 were shared with the children. Wearing's work (Figures 3.1 and 3.2) focuses on discovering details about individuals and the artist has said:

> *When I look at how people use brands I often think how we use them to tell the public world a story about who we are: or rather how we wish to be perceived by others. They are a way of protecting our private selves from disclosure.*

Figures 3.1 and 3.2 Signs that Say What You Want Them To Say and Not Signs that Say What Someone Else Wants You To Say by Gillian Wearing, courtesy Maureen Paley, London

The class explored the images, considering how they present the difference between public and personal personas. They discussed the complexity of their own identities and feelings, through rich exploratory talk: looking at others' perspectives, trying out new possibilities and forming opinions. Following this conversational journey, children were encouraged to create their own image in the style of Gillian Wearing. Teachers, parents, teaching assistants and even the new headteacher participated and a collage was created and displayed in the classroom (Figure 3.3).

Figure 3.3 5P's Wearing: class art based on work by artist Gillian Wearing

Class teacher: *I'm learning it's ok not to be perfect at everything.*
Parent/ TA: *Overworked and underpaid.*
Girl: *Give support to my father in hospital.*
Boy: *I want more responsibility.*
Boy: *Helping other people makes me happy.*
Boy: *I want my grandad to be happy not sad.*
Boy: *Share peace with the rest of the world.*
Girl: *Give people peace.*

Some of the pupils' responses were personal, linked to their first hand experiences; others demonstrated concerns about the wider world. The portraits were seen as a communication of themselves, disclosing aspects of the children's personality. All of the responses were open, exposing thoughts and opinions which the children felt confident enough to share. The class and teacher were becoming partners in their learning; showing interest in and asking questions of each other and beginning to articulate the different layers to personality, not always visible to others.

Then they were not just talking about themselves, there was an awareness of cross over, we were talking about community. The children began to see how our lives overlap, they mix and match.

During the next sessions children considered their daily lives in more detail. Katie wanted them to think about the places and people and how they contribute to who they are. Using world maps, the class placed artefacts, foods and images on the countries they were from. They then annotated the maps with examples of language from different parts of the world (Figure 3.4). The activity encouraged discussion about immigration and changing populations. Children began to ask themselves questions about what their lives might have been like if they had been born in different parts of the world: schools they might have gone to, houses they might have lived in. During these discussions, the teacher drew on the experience of pupils who had emigrated and they shared how their lives had changed.

Figure 3.4 World map activity

In order to consider the people, places, experiences and belongings that are important to them the teacher introduced a concentric circular diagram. Children placed themselves in the centre and things that were important to them in the outer circles in decreasing value.

Kaylie has named her family and home as most important (Figure 3.5). Grandparents, school, friends and money appear in the second circle. As the circles move away from the centre newer friends, food and members of the extended family are included. Kaylie's step family are also further away from the centre. Local community amenities such as the pizza shop, doctors, dentist are identified - the pizza shop is considered more important than the doctors!

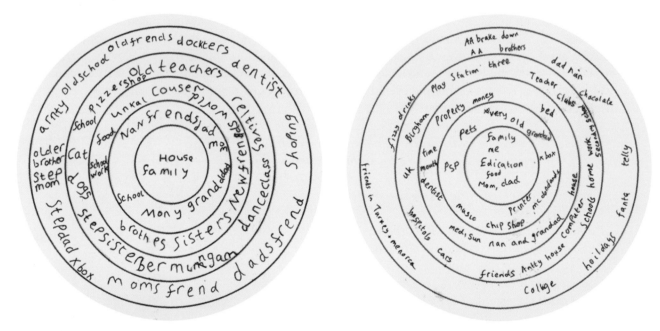

Figure 3.5 Kaylie's diagram: exploring aspects of her life, the people and places in it
Figure 3.6 Thomas' diagram
Figure 3.7 Anya's diagram

Thomas cites his parents, food and education as being most important to him (Figure 3.6). In the next circle he names fast food places, pets, PSP, X box, music and a favourite grandfather: 'very old granddad'. Thomas has also included favourite foods and places: Aunty's house, Birmingham, friends in Turkey and Menorca.

Anya identifies her family, mum and dad, siblings and pets as being most important to her (Figure 3.7). Next come friends, grandparents, school and her X box. She considers places in the next circle: McDonald's, the fish and chip shop, being part of the school drama club and other relatives. Her diagram combines family, friends, pets, belongings and the local community.

These diagrams enabled the children to consider the roles people, places and interests play in their day to day lives. They were beginning to think about the place of others in helping to shape and influence their identity and how these aspects interacted. The diagrams also demonstrated the complex nature of the family as many referred to the value placed on the relationships in step families.

Following on from this, identity mind maps allowed the children to further explore how their identity is shaped and influenced by family and those around them. The class discussed how people influence others through their genetic features, personalities and interests:

Kaylie: *I have hair like Aunty Jo when she was little.*
Diandra: *I like Take That because of my Aunty Louise.*
Hussain: *I speak Urdu because of my mum and I have my dad's nose.*
Aimee: *I'm named after someone in a film.*

Views of the family unit influenced contributions during this activity. A number of children were from one parent families, being raised by their mothers and this influenced their expectations for their own futures and family lives.

'I wanted parents and children to have one to one time to discuss their family and their lives.'

The concept of family trees was introduced through the use of BBC's *Who do you think you are?* programme and a website about a local family who have lived in the community since the 1800s. One child had recently suffered a bereavement. In sensitivity to this, Katie visited the family to discuss how best to approach the project. Parents and carers were invited into the classroom to enrich discussions and share family histories. Several of the parents took the opportunity to work with their children constructing family trees.

The workshop encouraged families to talk to each other, providing a learning experience that was real. Children were fascinated by each other's photographs and memories and this allowed opportunities to listen, share, respond to and question their peers. A relationship of greater respect and trust was developing between the members of the class. The children felt comfortable to explore themselves. In opening up they became vulnerable but trusted that the classroom was a place of security to share or withhold information as they chose.

A grandmother bought in bags and bags of things.

'Each piece is unique to the child. It is their identity and how they see themselves. It's what they value the most.'

In preparation for writing, children worked to explore the design and composition of paper based information texts. In groups they analysed texts with a focus on design: layout, use of images and typographical features. They were encouraged to formulate personal responses to non-fiction. Children created writing frames based on double page spreads, deconstructing multimodal texts (Figure 3.8). After reading several non-chronological reports, the class worked to identify language features and discussed aspects of style and tone. They used these experiences to create success criteria for non-chronological reports.

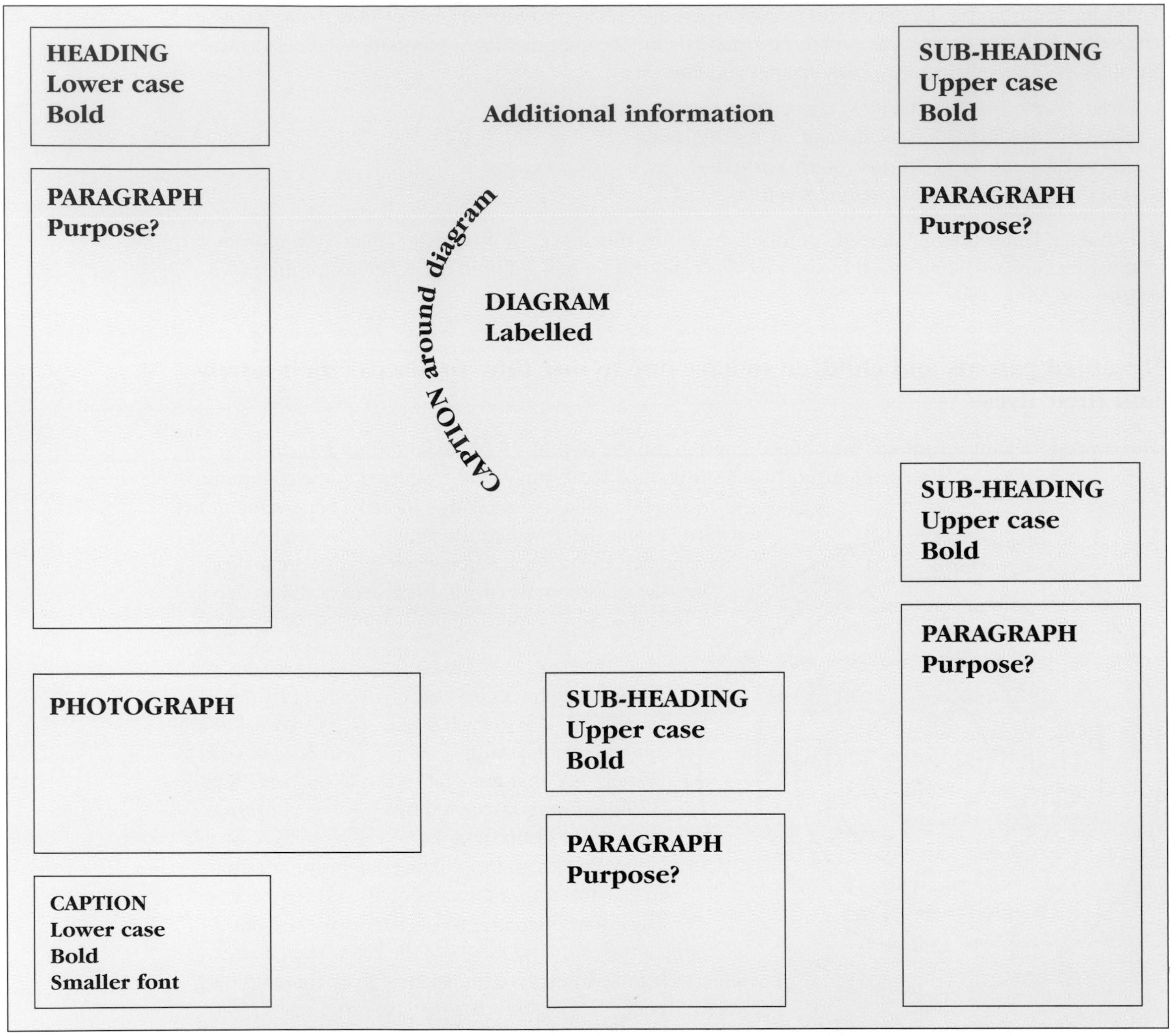

HEADING
Lower case
Bold

Additional information

SUB-HEADING
Upper case
Bold

PARAGRAPH
Purpose?

PARAGRAPH
Purpose?

CAPTION around diagram

DIAGRAM
Labelled

SUB-HEADING
Upper case
Bold

PARAGRAPH
Purpose?

PHOTOGRAPH

SUB-HEADING
Upper case
Bold

PARAGRAPH
Purpose?

CAPTION
Lower case
Bold
Smaller font

Above: Figure 3.8 An example of a writing frame based on a double page spread from a children's information text

The children moved on to compose multimodal non-chronological reports: All about me. They were given freedom to select information from earlier activities and create individual writing frames based on models read. Digital cameras were taken home so that children could photograph aspects of their life and select images for their reports. They identified sections, information and layout of their final composition. Katie used modelled and shared approaches to support writing of the report. Throughout the writing process, the children were encouraged to return to their writing, editing and redrafting of work using the success criteria.

'Every individual reflected on their identities - what made them who they are.'

I hardly ever have to step in - in terms of conflict or an issue... this is down to acceptance. That is what they've developed through this, an acceptance.

Following the project Katie reflected: 'they got a lot from having others to cement and share their experiences.' The project enabled the children to understand the complex nature of identity. They valued learning about themselves and others and shared private aspects of their lives with confidence. This had an impact on their self-esteem and enthusiasm for learning. Teacher, adults and children were partners in learning and there was an ethos of understanding and collaboration. By encouraging independence and choice in the final written outcome the teacher provided opportunities for the children's voices to be heard.

> *It got them to consider their lives, identities and who they are.*

One of the school's aims is to develop a meaningful curriculum. By engaging parents and linking the children's home and school lives, Katie showed the young people that their identities, experiences, knowledges and artefacts are valued in school. She used a range of different approaches to make connections so that the learning was authentic. In doing so she was able link the school curriculum to the children's everyday lives and the local community.

'We are a changing school'

As a development of the project, Katie has worked with a small team to explore how pedagogies and practices can be further developed across the school. They have planned and taught teaching sequences which endeavour to link the children's home lives and local community to curriculum requirements and link literacy to other areas, providing opportunities to develop talk and writing skills. The literacy subject leader is closely involved in these developments to ensure talk, reading and writing is effectively and meaningfully integrated in all learning.

> *If I hadn't backed off, I'd have missed the point. We've evaluated every step of the way, the importance of family, of family history, of the community.*

Raising attainment in literacy and developing purposeful opportunities to write is central to the school's improvement plan. Year 5's non-chronological reports reveal the sense of purpose for writing. By giving the children choice, the teacher motivated the writers who chose to share different aspects of themselves with their readers. Chanai drew on the parent workshop and chose to write about her family tree:

> *They have thought about it... what's left is what they value, the honesty, the discussions.*

> *A huge percentage of my family come from Jamaica; they all originate from different parts of Jamaica such as: Kingston, St Elizabeth and Port-Antonio. My great-grandparents were Thomas and Maisie M... (my granddad's parents) and Robert and Isilda H... (my Nan's parents). My Nan and granddad called Clifton (Cliff for short) and Verona M... Some of my family live in America, Spain, Jamaica or England. Most of them come from my father's side. Despite having loads of family I hardly ever see most of them. If my grandparents hadn't moved to England in the 1930s to find work my family would probably never have been here.*

She also includes a section on her hobbies, accompanied by images:

> *In my spare time (which I have a lot of usually) I like to either pick up a book and read it until I'm supposed to do something else or ask for my DS or laptop. When I feel like it I play on the Wii. I only got into acting and singing in my extra time when I started doing drama club on Saturdays with people I know.*

In one paragraph, Hussain also describes his hobbies:

> *I am Hussain and I like playing football and playing police games in the garden or elsewhere. I like getting creative at home by drawing; my favourite subject is drawing cars. I have made a big play site out of a small piece of cardboard and a big piece of cardboard. It has come out amazingly and it's great fun to play on. I'm also a cricket fan and have got a great cricket bat to play with my brother in the garden.*

Taylor has chosen to write a section describing her relationship with her dad:

To me my dad is really special. He likes to give me as much money as he can. He's very nice and we love each other very much. When we are together we spend time watching films and going to the park to play.

Faiza describes her likes and dislikes:

I have a very bad habit of biting my nails and I'm trying to stop. I love to spend time with my family and friends. I also love my mum's curries with rice and chapati. I like McDonald's too but I hate vinegar and tomatoes. I'm also very competitive.

The writing demonstrates that children have drawn on different aspects of the teaching sequence for their reports and have invited the reader into their lives, revealing their understanding of their own identity. As the teacher concludes: 'each piece is unique to the child. It is their identity and how they see themselves. It's what they value the most.'

Conclusion

When planning the unit both Katie and Rebecca wanted to look for ways to be creative with time, place, people and pedagogies. The approaches chosen: using art, lots of talk, world maps and deconstruction of real texts developed the children's confidence to share and explore as they collaborated with and learnt from each other. The teacher took risks and tried approaches that were unfamiliar: learning took place in a range of locations and involved different people. Lessons did not always sit neatly into a subject specific box, for example literacy or art. The children's oral and written work was shared with real audiences and time for reflection and self-assessment was planned into the sessions. As a result the teacher reflected that learners were more committed and independent.

Acknowledgements

With thanks to Katie Palmer and year 5 of Yardley Wood community primary school.

Grateful thanks to Gillian Wearing and Maureen Paley, London, for permission to use images.

Reflections

- How is your curriculum linked to the local community?
- How might you be more flexible with your use of time, place, people and teaching approaches?
- How might you bring out of school life experiences into the classroom?

UKLA

Garfield's global garden: talking, learning, growing

Daniella Sacco, Rebecca Thomas and Nirvana Culora

As the garden grows, so does the gardener Nora Jarbou[1]

Garfield is a primary school in Arnos Grove in the London borough of Enfield. The school has a children's centre on site. Like many schools in the borough, Garfield primary school's population is both multiethnic and multilingual, the largest group being those with East European, African or Turkish heritage. The large majority of pupils speak English as an additional language. Mobility is a challenge with a high proportion of pupils entering or leaving the school other than at usual times. The school has long regarded their ethnic and linguistic diversity as positive and tries to embrace this diversity in learning and teaching. An opportunity for this arose with the development of the Garfield global garden, the seeds for which were sown at an Enfield LA training session about developing a culturally inclusive curriculum. Daniella Sacco, a teacher at Garfield school, attended the training led by Rebecca Thomas and Nirvana Culora and the school received an incentive of £500 to support school based action.

The school lies in a built-up area made up of some temporary housing and tower blocks. Families do not have easy access to green spaces and gardens. Children's outdoor experiences are limited and this is sometimes reflected in their language and literacy. At the time of developing the garden, one of the school priorities on their school plan, was to develop the outside environment to become more welcoming and attractive, providing both sensory and cross curricular learning experiences. Another priority was to ensure that pupils had more opportunities to apply their literacy skills in subjects across the curriculum for a range of purposes. Stories about gardening and growing and hands on experience were planned to enrich pupils' learning and language experiences and extend vocabulary and structures through reading and oracy activities.

A culturally inclusive curriculum

In developing a culturally inclusive curriculum, teachers, pupils and communities embark on a journey where they can draw on one another's experience and expertise to create a curriculum that represents all our stories. By opening up thinking, everyone can explore a global perspective, developing young people's interest in the world and their relationship with it. One aspect of the culturally inclusive curriculum training encourages participants to think about areas of the curriculum that could be transformed. The project at Garfield was informed by the following criteria for planning a culturally inclusive curriculum:

- include skills, experiences and expertise of parents and members of the local community
- draw on pupils' cultural and linguistic experiences
- highlight shared values across cultures and celebrate difference.

The project

There was a particular piece of the school site which was grey and barren, but had the potential for a makeover as well as providing valuable outdoor learning space. This was in a contained part of the school that could be easily accessed by all the children for most of the day throughout the year. The aims were to:

- include pupils in planning their learning
- plan multi-sensory, experiential activities through which to develop skills, subject knowledge and understanding
- provide outdoor experiences which mirror and complement indoor provision as well as extending children's learning in order to offer opportunities which are not available indoors
- offer the possibility to work on a much larger scale
- increase involvement of the parent group in the life of the school and their children's learning, particularly, minority ethnic parents.

Building the garden

Daniella describes the development of the project:

> I wanted to do a gardening club because I couldn't bear looking out of the window at that awful space. I put up a photo of the site in the school entrance hall asking the children for ideas of what could be done to make a garden (Figure 4.1).

Figure 4.1 Getting ideas for the garden

> In twenty minutes the sheet was full of suggestions and names of people who could come and help. The children sketched ideas of things they would like to see in the garden and this is genuine inclusion because children of all ages and abilities were interested and involved. We had different age groups from throughout the school: parents, teachers and teaching assistants all set about transforming that outside area into a learning space that all classes could use (Figures 4.2 and 4.3). First the space needed painting and decorating. A local DIY store donated paint and adult and child volunteers came forward through calls of support via posters, newsletters items and notices in assembly developed and produced by the children. The project really gathered momentum as soon as the splash of colour appeared on the walls and as a result even more volunteers came forward. In no time at all our garden had begun to take shape based on the children's ideas.

Figures 4.2 and 4.3 Transformation

> The children talked about 'our garden' at home and a variety of plants, flowers, packets of seeds and containers began to materialise and the project took off like wildfire. We had to be resourceful because although we had received £500, the money wouldn't stretch very far so, for example, when I saw that some shelves were being thrown out we rescued them, transformed them into boxes, lined them and filled them with soil. Other members of the school community were helpful in providing extra resources. We had a relief caretaker – Jim - who was an absolute godsend because he had his own allotment and brought us in a lot of plants and Fanoulla, who is a school cleaner, brought plants as well; it got the school community involved. The range of insects, flowers and plants: aubergine, peppers, courgettes, sweetcorn, strawberries and herbs generated a lot of discussion and interest throughout the school (Figures 4.4. and 4.5).

> To date the activities have included sensory experiences, observational drawings, talk including discussions about living things as well as opportunities for questioning and collaboration. The children also learn about

> what sustainable development means in a context familiar to them. Learning in the garden has had a positive effect on particular children's behaviour, interest and self-esteem. There have been two main ways in which the children have been involved: through gardening club which took place after school each week till the end of the summer term and in individual classes, particularly my own.

Figure 4.4 My Mummy makes dolma with these leaves
Figure 4.5 Can we eat these green tomatoes?

Learning across the curriculum

At Garfield the global garden is seen as part of the curriculum and not as an add-on. It also supports putting what we teach in a global context. It was intended that the garden should not only be a focus for after school clubs but also a learning zone for individual classes to use the space for different areas of the curriculum. One class grew herbs as part of a project on the Tudors so we now have a herb area. It has been used for science, language and literacy, numeracy and ICT as well as providing opportunities for PSHE. If any teachers feel they don't have time to get involved in the gardening element I encourage them just to go in to the garden and read. There is a table there and the parents donated the canopy so classes can go out there occasionally to do Guided Reading. The garden can be used in many different ways (Figures 4.6 and 4.7).

Figures 4.6 and 4.7 Working and learning in the garden

With my year 2 class I based instructional writing on the work we had done in the garden - how we prepared the soil and planted. I have collected a range of books about gardens, plants and insects that the children consult readily as well as looking for information on the internet. We grew sunflowers and in numeracy and art we measured them, sketched them and learned about Vincent van Gogh. But some of the best learning came by chance. One morning I found that all the broccoli had been eaten by little caterpillars. I nearly cried. But I got the viewfinders and minibugs equipment and told the children what had happened. They set about bug hunting and collected thirty two caterpillars that we kept in a special box in the classroom and fed with leaves. The children kept watching them but after one weekend we came in and saw little piles of eggs in the box. I discovered from the internet that a parasite fly had planted their eggs inside the caterpillars and that they hatch out of the caterpillar while it is still alive. I told the children about it and although they were rather upset at first we used it as a discussion of natural processes. We talked about how all living things need to eat and the children learned about the life cycle of this parasitic fly. We managed to keep six caterpillars which developed into cocoons and then hatched into cabbage white butterflies. The children fed them with a sugary solution and the whole day they were on butterfly watch until we released them - over the other side of the school away from the garden! It made our science come alive. I was so excited. They were excited.

Language development

This hands on authentic learning has led to the children in my class learning not just facts about plants and insects but developing specific language to explain their ideas. For example, two children, Denzel and Andy, were seen taking ladybirds off the plants and when they were asked about it they said 'we're putting them where the blackflies are…' On another occasion, instead of screaming when a bee came along, Saida, a usually excitable girl, said: 'calm down… we need them because they pollinate the flowers…' using that scientific language. As an outcome of the parasite fly experience I had taught the children about the different sections of an insect and we made them with papier maché and looked at National Geographic videos on the internet. One boy who struggles with learning was able to explain about the life cycle and structure of the parasite fly and a couple of the children went and explained to the head and deputy about what had been happening. The children began to talk like experts using specialist vocabulary and phrases but I also noticed that they have become better at taking turns and working together. I have heard children saying to each other 'let me show you…' or 'try this…' - talking in ways they might not have used before.

Across the school as a whole one of the main gains from the garden has been in the children's use of language. There has been a massive amount of communication - with peers and with adults all talking about what and where to plant, how the plants are doing, how to care for them and what can be cooked with particular fruit and vegetables. There have been particular gains for bi- or multilingual children. The teacher with particular responsibility for Ethnic Minority Achievement, took the children into the garden and they were able to use their own languages to describe the colours, name the fruit and vegetables and talk about the kinds of food they ate at home.

The children could often be observed talking excitedly in their home language as well as in English. We have a big multicultural population and there were some key moments of dialogue, for example, about the

dolma (Figure 4.3) which Skevi the TA who supports me cooked with the children. But there was also a lovely conversation over the strawberries, donated by a parent, where the children were saying: 'in my country they're called this… and: 'in my country they're called that…', making comparisons, noticing that some were quite like the words they would use and others quite different (Figures 4.8 and 4.9).

Figures 4.8 and 4.9 What do you call a strawberry?

Starting from concrete experience gave the children had something to talk about. Even a child who lacks self-confidence talked quite freely about all the processes he had seen: planting, growing, picking, cooking, eating. I had never heard him talk so much. Many of the learning gains have been in motivation, for example, a boy who was often aggressive has learned that he has to be more careful and thoughtful if he wants to work in the garden.

Working with parents

Many children have brought their parents to see the garden and share their enthusiasm about it. It has been important to encourage the parental community to become more active inside the school and have a genuine chance of participating. I still want to make the garden more of a collaboration between families and the school. There are some parents who do want to do more: not all of them want to work with the children. Other parents have said they'll come in and paint. At a recent parents evening all the parents there were asked to fill out a questionnaire about how they would like to see the garden develop and what they might like to do. It's a chance to get other teachers involved as well. It's a gradual development of a culture - to help parents gain the confidence to take up things in the school. Parents need to make it their own so that they'll be more committed.

Next steps

The first year was rather trial and error as we all learned about the pleasures and hazards of setting up a garden. The next phase is to involve more classes gradually and to involve more parents. We shall buy a shed because if the project is to become part of the culture of our school we need the proper resources, particularly a place where we keep the gloves, the tools and other equipment. We also need a tap installed because watering has been a problem. I've found myself asking colleagues to pass watering cans of water through the classroom windows in order to get enough water on the plants!

In the autumn term of the second year of the garden the children in year 2 planted bulbs. Gardening club was only held for three weeks and in spring the club will start again. Three weeks club participation will be allocated to each year group so that the planting will be phased. There are now extra planting boxes linked to each classroom so there will be a spread of responsibility.

Conclusion

Looking back, the Garfield global garden project has achieved all that we set out to do - and more. As far as developing cultural inclusion is concerned, we have been able to draw on the skills, experiences and expertise of parents although there is more we can do and we still have to involve members of the community around the school. The project has been powerful in building on and developing the children's cultural and linguistic experiences and, perhaps more by accident than design, we have been able to share experiences across cultures and celebrate difference.

In terms of learning aims, the children have been centrally involved in planning their own learning - making the garden, growing and enjoying the fruits (and vegetables!) of their own labour. There have been many opportunities for multi-sensory, experiential activities which have developed the children's skills, knowledge and understanding, sometimes in unexpected ways. Outdoor provision has enabled learning which was not previously possible as well as complementing classroom learning. Gradually, parents are becoming more involved in the life and learning of the school, particularly, minority ethnic parents whose gardening and cooking expertise have been greatly appreciated. Apart from these valuable achievements, the children's standards of speaking and listening as well as their literacy have improved significantly through their involvement in Garfield's global garden. We have every hope that these gains will continue and increase.

Do

- Encourage all year groups and other adults to get involved
- Delegate
- Respond to children's interests; use them as opportunities for learning across the curriculum
- Establish rules about working in the garden: formulate them with the children
- Embrace the opportunity to teach and learn outside
- Approach local businesses to support the project
- Try as far as possible to buy child friendly equipment
- Enjoy and go with the flow
- Take lots of photos for use as a visual diary

Don't

- Forget to carry out a risk assessment

Useful resources

The Royal Horticultural Society (RHS) have a very useful website The RHS Campaign for School Gardening with a wealth of advice about health and safety, fundraising and sponsorship and monthly gardening tips. http://apps.rhs.org.uk/schoolgardening/ accessed 29th November 2011

Morrison's supermarket also have a 'Let's Grow' scheme with growing guides and giveaways of equipment http://www.morrisons.co.uk/letsgrow/ accessed 29th November 2011

Notes

[1] Nora Jarbou writes for 'La Gazetta Italiana' an Italian language newspaper and website published in The United States of America. Accessed on November 27th 2011
http://www.lagazzettaitaliana.com/gardengrows.aspx

Reflections

- Who might you work with to develop a project like this in your school?
- How could such a project enrich your school provision/curriculum?
- How would you involve the children in all stages?

Literacy and identity:
making the invisible visible
Winifred Burke

South Petherton junior school, Somerset, is a smaller-than-average-sized 7-11 rural junior school which in 2007 faced an unexpected change of leadership due to the sudden death of the headteacher. When appointed, the new incumbent shared her plans with governors as to how she would like to bring about change as she recognised that literacy teaching had been too focused on knowledge, skills and under-standing at the expense of creativity. Teaching and learning were unequal partners in the classroom. Standardised assessment test results (SATs) in writing were also lower than expected. This became the focus for our exploration and at this point, as Chair of Governors and literacy governor with experience in educational research, I became actively involved in the process.

When we began our action research into children's writing[1] we little thought that the invisible factors that became visible would prove so important in informing our cohesion policy and practice. Almost all the pupils are of White British heritage. Only a few speak English as an additional language. An average percentage of pupils have special educational needs and/or disabilities, including physical, moderate and specific learning difficulties. With new housing in the village, the school roll has risen over the past five years with increasing numbers of pupils entering the school after the beginning of year 3. This has resulted in a need for teachers and governors to look more closely at the demographic mix in the community and how teaching and learning are affected by social and cultural factors existing outside the school.

Years spent responding to outside initiatives had resulted in teachers growing compliant and fearful of risk taking. The focus on meeting targets had also resulted in less time to talk to children and parents. Literacy appeared as something that was done to learners rather than with them. We were dismayed when the year 3 teacher complained that children in her class had no ideas of their own when writing and that whilst most year 6 children achieved above expectations in the standard assessment tests many left the school not enjoying reading or writing.

When we began our study the headteacher taught the year 4 class for half the week and fulfilled her leadership and managerial roles for the rest of the time. Inclusion was planned for in terms of gender, ability and special needs and there was little consideration of the effect of out of school literacy practices on children's learning. Black *et al.* (2000: 7) wrote that: 'teachers do need to present content but not exclusively; sometimes instead becoming leaders of an exploration.' This was behind our thinking in the action research.

Key concepts

Literacy is deeply related to power and identity:

- those of us who are literate can exercise 'power over' (Kreisberg, 1992) our lives more than those who are not
- those who have the power to define what counts as valid and valuable literacy hold the greatest power of all.

In recent years, in England, it has been government policy and practice not to trust teachers but to exercise power over schools and this in turn has encouraged teachers to exercise power over their pupils rather than share 'power with' them (*ibid.*, p 85). This has led to rather instrumental literacy interventions and a denial of the complexities involved. Kreisberg distinguishes between what he terms coercive 'power over' based on domination, and 'power with', which is 'characterised by collaboration, sharing and mutuality' (*ibid.*, p.61)[2]. Whilst the exercise of power is not unidirectional or uncontested, neither is access to power equal either in the home or at school. If parents or teachers deny the child a voice they are not only exerting 'power over' in the present but setting in motion the expectations and actions that will perpetuate the practice in the future. A consciousness of issues of power and identity and a view of learning which sets the establishment of 'power with' as an aim seems to be a prerequisite for developing effective cohesive literacy practice. To move aims into practice teachers would need to uncover their pupils' funds of existing knowledge (Moll *et al.*, 1992) and 'offer ways to deepen their understandings and broaden their perspectives on their own and others' lives' (p 90). They might also need to understand the value of 'seeing their learners differently rather than making assumptions about what learners can do - or not do' (Comber, 2001: 129). Shifting assumptions and expectations such as these often mean making invisible literacy practices visible, since:

- children's identities are neither fixed nor singular but constantly changing, multiple and complex
- recognising the plurality and ambiguous nature of children's literate identities places an added responsibility on teachers and parents
- at a time of great technological change discontinuity between the school curriculum and out of school textual experiences can widen the gap between learners' expectations of texts and their uses and pleasures.

As Kress (2006) writes 'one of the major problems for young people in schools, is the gap between the expectations that they bring from their world and the expectations that exist in the school from a former world' (p 294). The following case studies show how asking children to share their personal interests with their peers and teachers brings some of their previously invisible experiences into the light.

Year 4 case studies[3]

To illustrate the importance of taking account of social and cultural factors in planning for inclusion in literacy we share findings from two identified gifted and talented and two potentially higher attaining children. They are all of White British heritage. Their teachers selected them because they perceived in them problems which if unresolved might prevent the children from reaching their full potential in school. Zak and Belle were on the gifted and talented register; he for sport, she for drama. Zak was considered 'a puzzlement' by his teacher because of his inconsistent attitude and commitment to achieve well in literacy. Whilst Belle was acknowledged as a good all-rounder, her teacher was concerned that her lack of confidence in her own ability to reach the targets set was slowing her progress. John and Rainbow were potentially higher attaining pupils but John was a reluctant speaker in class, preferring to nod his head or point when asked to answer a question, whilst Rainbow's low self esteem was seriously affecting her learning. All four children were targeted for the higher level 5 in reading, writing and English by the end of year 6.

Zak and Belle *(year 1 of the project)*

Zak and Belle both come from comfortable, middle class homes. He lives with his mother and dad and older brother. His mother has a higher degree and works as an engineer. She has passed on her love for and success in mathematics to Zak. The boy shares his father's passion for sport and has been selected as a member of the football academy in the nearby town. Dad and Zak regularly read the sports pages in the local newspaper. Whenever we observed Zak outside lessons, he was always actively involved in group activities.

Belle is an only child living with her mother and father. Her mother is a social worker. Her father is a teacher. Both her parents love reading; mother reads fiction and dad non-fiction. Like her mother, Belle plays the violin. The family are very keen on outdoor activities. Whenever we observed Belle either in or outside lessons she naturally assumed the role of teacher with her peers. Her mother felt that her daughter seemed happiest when she had an audience.

In the course of our interview with Zak it became clear that he has a good vocabulary and can express himself clearly. His account of his busy and interesting home life seems to leave very little time for writing outside school. He prefers his mother to read to him because: 'she [gets] through the book quicker.' His mother confirms that the only time she could remember him writing voluntarily at home was when he wanted to improve his handwriting and in that task he had been very diligent. Zak is more enthusiastic about reading non-fiction books such as *Microscopic Monsters* than fiction. He doesn't like the amount of time that is spent in planning before writing in school, dislikes targets and says he finds difficulty in sitting still on the carpet and listening to the teacher. In talking to Zak we noticed that he was keener to comment on and evaluate points already made than to offer new ideas. When we interviewed his mother she admitted to this trait in herself. The only time Zak became enthusiastic about school literacy was when he recalled a writer of football stories coming to talk to the class. He had persuaded his mother to buy the book, read it himself and could recall the content months after the event.

Belle was equally articulate during interview. Her ambition is to be an actress. She attends weekly drama classes in a nearby town and has clearly learned a great deal about stagecraft from doing so. She said: 'it makes me more confident in acting because there are people there that I don't know and I have to act in front of them and you get better and more confident.' Her mother confirmed that Belle writes regularly at home: 'has lots of good ideas but rarely completes anything'. She was taken to places of interest from an early age: 'encouraged to do projects… in fact our house is full of unfinished projects.' Belle seems particularly interested in books about other people's lives that are different from her own. Her favourite author is Jacqueline Wilson. She says that she gets ideas for writing from books and films: 'I've just read a spy book and now I would like to write a story about a spy.' Belle's mother confirmed her teacher's view that Belle was: 'above the standard level for just about everything' but her 'confidence in some subjects isn't as good as others… say her confidence in her mathematics ability.' Belle agrees: 'I'm usually quite confident to meet teacher targets but sometimes I might not be able to do it…but usually I can.'

We began our work with Belle and Zak by introducing journal writing in their class in order to give the children more control over the content of what they were writing. We also tapped into their existing stores of knowledge by asking them to write about their favourite place. Zak wrote about the place in Southern France where he and his family lived for a year and where he had been to school (Figure 5.1). Belle had more difficulty in choosing one place and instead wrote about three in Australia that she and her family had visited on holiday. However, she identified her favourite piece of writing as part of a ghost story she had written (Figure 5.2).

Figure 5.1
Extract from
Zak's first
journal entry:
My favourite place

> ## My favourite place
>
> My favourite place is France because while I was in France for 6 months with my Mum, my Dad, my brother and myself, we did lots of interesting things like go ice skating and we went to school there.
>
> At are house in France the people that owned the house were quite old and when the man was younger it was really sad because a cow's horn went into his eye and took his eye out so now he has a plastic eye to replace it and so now he can only see with one eye. He owned a big area of space and in that space he had chickens and rabbits. The rabbits he used to kill and then eat the rabbits until there was only one or two left and so they could give birth and then he would let them grow a little bit so he did the same again each time. The man was called Monsieur Bouchet. Monsieur Bouchet has lived in Chorges all of 82 years of his life which hasn't ended yet.
>
> Sometimes we had snow in the garden but most of the snow fell on the mountain tops. We didn't have very much rain so me and my brother could play lots of football in the garden together. The rain that we did have it all dried up quite quickly because the air was so dry so the washing could dry in about an hour on every day that it wasn't raining in winter which obviously wasn't very often that it rained. We used to get lots of nutella from the Super Marche and I loved the peaches.

Figure 5.2
Extract from
Belle's ghost story:
the writing she
was most
proud of

> It's happened again. Ever since moving here two weeks ago I have had a shiver running down my spine. At exactly 4 o'clock a ghostly shadow quavers through the garden gate. It reaches far across the flagstones in the searing heat.
>
> In the short time we have been at Miller's End it has been made clear that it needs a lot of work. The whole village is dilapidated though to be fair it was built in the 18th century. The walls can barely be seen for the cracks and ancient ivy. I'm convinced that there is something not right.
>
> I stare around the room I have picked; it is filled with boxes and so eerie that I decide to go outside to listen to the beautiful birdsong. I trudge outside! That's strange it's completely silent, no bird song at all. I approach an old bush then I feel a cold sharp tap on my shoulder; it is so light I wouldn't have noticed it if it wasn't so cold. I swing round and standing in front of me is Billy the garden boy, smiling and looking through his curtain of black hair.
>
> "Something bothering you Miss Evelyn?" Billy asks in an old fashioned way.

Journal writing provoked an immediate change in Zak's attitude and motivation. This was noticed by his mother as he changed from a boy who rarely wrote at home to one about whom his mother asked: 'What have you done to my son? He's a different person... it's hard to get him to put his writing project down!' Freed from learning intentions and success criteria he worked in his preferred way: 'I like getting on with things… just thinking when I'm writing it down and when I've thought of a thought just write it down…'

Belle not only completed her writing about Australia but we noticed how driven she was to produce writing of a high standard. As she read her account to the class she constantly edited her entry on the page to better express her feelings about the place. Maybe we reasoned it was a need to perform (Dweck, 1989) and a fear of failure that was adversely affecting her self-confidence. From what we had learned from each child we recognised the need to develop learning goals that are self-generated rather than imposed upon them by others.

We asked Zak to produce a report on what it was like to belong to a football academy so that other pupils in his class would understand what was involved. We knew that Belle's family were due to spend a year in New Zealand when her father took up a teacher exchange post. Her challenge was to produce an account of her English school to show to her new classmates. Interestingly Zak chose to plan and produce a PowerPoint™ presentation as most suited to engage the year 4 children's interest and Belle chose to make a video recording of the school. They both received one to one adult support in the time leading up to the presentations. It was conducted in the form of reflective dialogues, with the teacher acting as a 'guide on the side' rather than a 'sage on the stage' (Blatchford, 2003:164). The planning and emphasis on skill training from Zak's football academy was very evident during these sessions as he checked his own progress and ticked off completed tasks as the deadline drew nearer. Belle was equally involved in the task as she planned to use her dad's video recorder and decided how she would try to capture the important features of the school.

In the July after the project started, Zak delivered a quality presentation before his peers, teachers and mother and also fully answered their questions about training routines and the importance of high and low carbohydrate diets for football training. Belle's video proved less sophisticated because it was in unedited form. Her teacher said: 'I expected Belle's to be better than Zak's and it wasn't.' What she had forgotten was that whilst Zak and Belle had had many opportunities in school to learn about making PowerPoint™ presentations neither had had the opportunity to edit the footage from a video camera. Belle's self-esteem suffered from this experience as she burst into tears and needed to be consoled by her teacher.

It would be wrong to say that this short intervention changed Zak. He is still a boy who likes to be active and when given the choice between completing his written work in class and taking a break with friends, then writing proves his second choice. Nevertheless both his teachers and mother have a greater understanding of what he is capable of and how to make the most of his interests. After twelve months in New Zealand, Belle returned to the school as a more confident girl. During this time she had been exposed to a school culture very different from our own. Rather than worrying about performing against external criteria she now understood that the best learning is internally generated and controlled. She had been trained in using and editing video film and was keen to point out what she had done wrong in the original filming.

Tapping into these two children's existing funds of knowledge gave us a sound base from which to plan individualised programmes of work in order to challenge and advance their learning. The head teacher said: 'it's been great having time to listen to children's voices after years of setting targets and jumping through hoops.' Although she still admitted that: 'teaching knowledge and skills and assessing in a linear progression is a fact of life in primary schools' hearing these children's voices focused her mind on the need for better links between home and school literacy.

John and Rainbow (second year of the project)

John and Rainbow have fewer advantages in their home lives than Zak and Belle. John lives with his mother, father and younger brother. His mother is at home full time and at the time of the study was expecting her third child. Rainbow lives with her mother and four older siblings. Mother is struggling to support her family. Rainbow's father has left home. Unlike Zak and Belle these children are not well travelled. John's family don't take holidays whilst Rainbow only occasionally visits her Welsh grandmother who is a published author.

When we interviewed John we found it very difficult to get more than monosyllabic answers to our questions, in marked contrast to the full written responses he gave in his reading log or when filling in a questionnaire about his preferred reading and writing tasks. He is a regular user of the local library. He prefers reading non-fiction such as 'Horrible Histories' to fiction although he enjoys science fiction. Rainbow proved very talkative but had short concentration spans. She admits using books as a means of escaping from home problems and particularly likes books about other people's relationships, for example, she enjoys reading Jacqueline Wilson's work. When questioned about what gave them most pleasure when writing, their answers revealed an insight into their perceptions of their own identities. Rainbow wrote: 'when my writing is praised I feel the centre of attention.' John wrote: 'I like writing stories and then reading back what I've wrote.'

Both children are interested in animals. Rainbow loves cats and knows a lot about how to look after them. John wants to be a zoologist and loves doing research either using the Internet or delving into library books. Figures 5.3 and 5.4 give examples of their preferences in writing fiction.

Since I Got Tiggy

Dear Scarlet Longfield last spring the most horrible thing happened to me. My cat went missing and I'm writing to you to tell you about her life. She is half Persian tortoise shell and here is her story.

It starts here, in a box, there was a tramp who was selling kittens I fell in love with one and one only. I took her home and named her Tiggy. Throughout her life she did everything with me and when I say everything I mean everything. We went on the computer together, we had tea together when I went to bed she would come with and lie next to me, when I was ill she would comfort me. Suddenly she became less active and her stomach became larger. On April the fifth, the sunniest day of spring, Tiggy disappeared. Later that month I found her nursing a whole litter of kittens. I named them Ash, Oren, Cadger and Envis.

> *Yours sincerely,*
> *Rainbow Cooper*

Dear Rainbow thank you for the latest heart warming letter, I enjoyed reading it. Would you mind if I used it in my book?

> *Yours sincerely,*
> *Scarlet Longfield*

Dear Scarlet Longfield, I am afraid to tell you this the day after I sent the letter Tiggy died and I am sorry that this letter is stained with tears.

> *Rainbow*

Figure 5.3 Extract from Rainbow's writing: 'Since I Got Tiggy'

> **Tobias as a Hawk**
>
> *Chapter One*
>
> *Tobias soared high above his field at dusk, at eight o'clock in midsummer, searching for prey. Eventually he saw a baby rabbit that was alone. He waited until he was at the right angle. Then he struck! He pierced through the air as fast as a bullet, being fired from a sniper. He caught it and then he felt warm blood dripping off his talons. He tore ravenously at the meat because he hadn't had anything to eat for three days. It was because he had been on a mission with a group called the Animorphs. They were made up of five children, Jake, their leader, Marco, Jake's best friend, Rachel, Jake's cousin, Cassie, Rachel's best friend and Tobias who was stuck as a hawk. They had been fighting yeerks, slug-like parasites that took over people's brains.*
>
> *Just then a green light filled the sky and a deafening whooshing sound surrounded Tobias which caused him to stop eating. Suddenly Tobias felt himself rising so he attempted to fly away. However, he couldn't fly. He thought to himself in awe, "Why am I not moving?" He stared up to find a massive UFO! It was circular and had green lights arranged in a circle around the middle of it. It was grey with black lines in a tartan pattern.*

Figure 5.4 Extract from John's writing inspired by K.A. Applegate's Animorph *stories: 'Tobias as a Hawk'*

We noted that John was much more talkative once the school day was over. He chatted constantly to his mother when she collected him after school. Her entry in his reading log confirmed that he talked freely when interested in the subject under discussion:

> *16th September 2009: John read in my company. We then discussed rainforests - what is happening to them? How sad it would be if they no longer existed. An emotional discussion.*

Rainbow's reading log was rarely filled in by her mother. When asked about this Rainbow admitted that the log was invading her private time away from her problems and that she actively dissuaded her mother from listening to her read at home. Rainbow showed her pride in her grandmother's prowess as an author by constantly referring to her work. When we put the two children together in a work situation, John had no problem in communicating with Rainbow, albeit very quietly, and she was very supportive of his privacy. We decided to set them a multimodal task and encourage collaborative working with minimal input from the teacher.

Two factors influenced this decision:

• both children had enjoyed the freedom that came from taking part in the recent school pantomime
• both liked using computers.

The higher level teaching assistant responsible for ICT indicated that she shared our approach: 'In ICT we are encouraged to get children to make their own choices and to think for themselves.' It was she who recommended that we use Microsoft Photo Story 3 with the children confirming: 'they have good IT skills and should cope with the programme easily.'

The shoe mystery

As the focus for role play as investigators, we placed two pairs of children's shoes on the carpet and encouraged John and Rainbow to solve the mystery of who the children were and what had happened to them. This led to the production of individual story boards. Using Photo Story 3 each child constructed their own account of what had happened to the children using video clips, digital images, text and music. John decided that the children had been abducted by aliens. Rainbow chose for them to be whisked away by the fairies. Once John was familiar with Photo Story 3 he taught Rainbow all that she needed to know about the process and we were left to observe their progress. When she needed atmospheric music she drew on electronic skills that she had learned in year 3. When John needed magnetic boots to counteract the effect of lack of gravity in the alien space ship he conducted a very efficient search of permitted internet sites in order to select the right image. They were independent learners for much of this time and the results were personal and engaging.

When Rainbow began she decided to leave the children with the fairies but by the time the text was complete she had decided, like John, to bring them home. What had happened that might have influenced her decision? Things were happier at home. Her mother had found a new partner and the family were going to move nearer to her grandmother in Wales.

Whilst most of the data collected in these case studies was qualitative we did use the Lawseq self-esteem questionnaire (Lawrence, 2006) before and after the intervention for both pairs of children in order to see whether there was any perceivable change brought about by the study. In Rainbow's case the change was very evident. Where John had originally scored 16 out of 24 and Rainbow had scored 8, at the end John had scored 18 and she had scored 17. An example we feel of changing home circumstances and successfully targeted school intervention.

Instead of seeing John and Rainbow in terms of what they could or could not do we looked at the effect of literacy on their complex and changing identities. We constantly tried to adjust our interventions in school to allow them space to take decisions, work from their strengths, make mistakes and learn to overcome difficulties. We also took account of their interests and behaviour outside school. Making their invisible lives visible helped us as teachers to better support their learning.

Next steps

Although the study made a difference to the learning of the children involved and was appreciated by their parents, we quickly recognised that it was having minimal impact on classroom practice. The headteacher commented: 'it's as if they are thinking this is something that we are doing with a few children but that it is not possible with twenty plus children in the normal classroom'. At this point she applied to the governing body to be relieved of her teaching commitment for six months in order to devote more time to monitoring teaching and learning with a view to changing mindsets in the school. This was duly granted.

Since then her focus on continuous professional development has slowly changed practice in the school. Talk precedes writing and peer and self-assessment inform learning. Through the introduction of home/ school projects, in each year group, some barriers have been broken down between out of school and in school learning. As a result children have more opportunities for self-generated learning goals rather than those imposed upon them by others.

Whilst we have come a long way since the project began in embedding cohesion at the level of the school we have also moved forward at the level of the wider national community by making links with an inner city multicultural school and the global community through links with an African school. There is still, however, work to do with the community in which the school is located. Broken homes and a wider socio-economic mix now concern us more than in the past. Whilst it would seem sensible to follow ethnographic researchers (Pahl, 2011) and visit homes to study the uses of literacy, concerns over health and safety issues and possible litigation are invisible factors that prevent teachers from making such visits or even driving a child home in their own car. As the headteacher said when Pahl's research was shared with her: 'Researchers might get away with it but not those working in schools.'

Conclusion

Through school meetings, newsletters and the school learning platform, staff and governors try to make clear to parents:

- why success in SATs is only one measure of achievement
- why hearing the child's voice is important
- why new learning based on existing knowledge lays the foundations for good literacy learning and identity.

We do this because parents and family members have more potential than teachers to facilitate children's literacy identities.

We may have come a long way in creating a better power balance in school and with some parents but the headteacher's response (July 2011) indicates that fear of external powers still imposes limits on the development of our cohesion practice within our local community.

Notes

[1] The research project was funded by The United Kingdom Literacy Association.
[2] An example of 'power over' schools was exemplified by the National Literacy Strategy which, whilst not statutory, acquired this status and was dominating classroom practice when we began this study.
[3] All names have been changed to preserve anonymity.

Reflections

- How might you draw upon children's literate identities to support your teaching and their learning?
- How might you provide further challenge for potentially high achieving pupils? What role might parents or carers play?
- How might the use of writing journals support learners in your classroom/ school?

Chapter 6 Looked After Children: supporting carers adopting a multimodal approach to literacy activities at home[1]

Petula Bhojwani

Background

This case study offers an insight into a local authority pilot project led by Petula Bhojwani and Liz Kitts which aimed to motivate and engage children in care with literacy at home. It outlines the programme of support with some reflections and gives a future schedule following the project's evaluation. During the period that this project was carried out there were approximately 700 children in care across Nottinghamshire, however, a focus group of twelve were selected for this pilot literacy initiative. All of these children were being looked after by foster carers and were not in residential care. Including two sets of twins, the group consisted of seven girls and five boys, ranging from Reception (5 years old) to year 8 (13 years old). There were many sensitive and complex factors and events that occurred during the project and a large degree of flexibility was required. At times group meetings had to be rearranged and replaced by the offer of individual consultant support and online communications in order to keep momentum and maintain relations.

Within the local authority there was a great deal of enthusiasm for this literacy initiative, as it would provide a direct link with the home environment. Furthermore, it was felt that there was huge potential in opening up dialogue between home and school as well as supporting both carers and teachers with motivating and engaging this vulnerable group. Following the success of a number of local authority literacy courses for schools on multimodality, this approach was adopted.

Engaging looked after children in literacy activities

The launch of the Looked After Children (LAC) project took place in March 2011. Headteachers were contacted prior to the event to gain their support and asked to select a member of staff to work alongside the carer. School colleagues who attended the day ranged from teaching assistants, class teachers, a support worker (referred to as a mentor) and a deputy head. A number of key figures from the local authority were also present at the launch including the senior educational psychologist, the head of the virtual school and educational welfare officers. Two education consultants led the launch; one specialised in literacy and the other in ICT. The main aim was to enthuse the young people in literacy and in particular increase their engagement in reading by adopting a multimodal approach[2]. A key message was that texts today are more than static words on a page - they can be visual, audio and pictorial - and the carers took part in a series of activities designed to illustrate how children's educational experiences can and should be more in line with their everyday encounters.

Project Sequence

The project was divided into three phases over six months:

Phase 1 Local authority training day to launch the pilot project:

- professional development for school staff and carers on a multimodal approach to literacy
- opportunity for carers and school to reflect on the child's literacy, behaviour and interests
- distribution of ICT resources and selected picture books for the children.

Phase 2 Development work within the home:

- carers introduce the children to the resources and picture books
- study support and literacy consultants keep in touch with carers and children via email and home, school or library visits made when requested
- children encouraged to send texts created over the Easter holiday period to the consultants
- hub meeting scheduled for carers to meet together to share progress.

Phase 3 Evaluation of the impact of the project:

- questionnaires completed by carers and children on their responses to the pilot project
- local authority representative meeting to evaluate the pilot project and highlight strengths and weaknesses in order to develop a revised programme for future groups of carers, schools and children.

Multi-layered picture books such as *Wolves* by Emily Gravett were studied to illustrate the different functions of picture and word on the page. Wolves was an excellent example of what some have called a 'faction' text as the images tell a story whilst the printed text provides facts about wolves. Together the meanings can be combined to make a sophisticated narrative which is enriched by knowledge about wolves.

Environmental print was also considered by examining leaflets. The activities showed that these texts are often confined to folded A4 pieces of paper and have been carefully designed to convey many messages through the layout of the page, sectioning, change of fonts, diagrams, framing of photographs etc. Discussions also progressed to the importance of promoting critical reading to encourage children to comment on how successfully messages have been conveyed using different techniques.

Talking photo albums (Figure 6.1) were introduced to the carers as a way of making a multimodal text. This resource provides the opportunity to include sound alongside image and printed text as the children can make recordings or narrations to accompany the page that they have created. The picture book *Archie's War* by Marcia Williams provided an interesting discussion on scrapbook design and creating multimodal texts which could include children's drawings, photographs, written combinations, artefacts and sound.

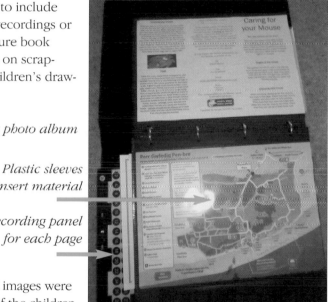

Figure 6.1 Example of a talking photo album

Screen texts were examined to stress that the children were very much part of a digital age. The understanding of design and layout were again emphasised as important to reading and the carers were shown how to transfer and transform images from picture books to the screen using Microsoft Photo Story 3. The picture book *Willy the Dreamer* by Anthony Browne was used to illustrate some of the features of Photo Story such as zooming in and out of an image to emphasise size and images were recreated by applying the sepia or black and white colour tools. All of the children were to receive a digital camera so that they would also be able to create their own images by uploading their pictures into Photo Story.

Plastic sleeves to insert material →

Recording panel for each page →

Making links with home and school

Baseline information was collected at the launch as this was an excellent opportunity for the carer and school representative to share and discuss thoughts and perceptions of the young people in their care. A Venn diagram was adapted from Pahl and Rowsell's (2005) work on identity and used by the participants to describe the children in the home and school settings (Figure 6.2). Time was also built into the day for carers and teachers to consider the young person's age, interests and ability in order to select three texts to take home from an array of multi-layered picture books purchased for the project (see Resources section).

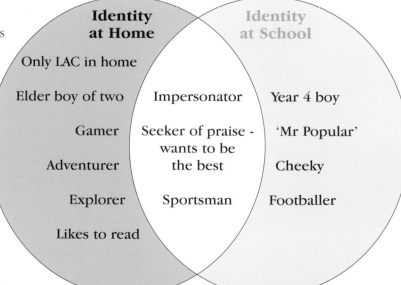

Figure 6.2 Example Venn diagram of carer and teacher perceptions of young person at home and at school

A carer's thoughts on a 7 year-old boy in her care:

> *Reluctant writer - imaginative and creative but reluctant to 'slog it out' with a pencil!*
>
> *Loves books, stories, but doesn't settle for long.*

Phase 2 Developing work within the home: consultant support

Two consultants remained in contact with the carers and children, one specialising in literacy the other in study support. With input from the consultants, each carer selected three of the following picture books (the year group bands were regarded flexibly due to the varying abilities of the children):

Reception - KS1
The Naughty Bus by Jan and Jerry Oke
The Odd Egg by Emily Gravett
A pop-up book of colour: Butterfly by Petr Horacek
Egg Drop by Mini Grey
Ape by Martin Jenkins
The Rabbit Problem by Emily Gravett

Years 3-4
Egg Drop by Mini Grey
Ape by Martin Jenkins
The Tunnel by Anthony Browne
Adventures of the Dish and the Spoon by Mini Grey
Free Fall by David Wiesner
Wolves by Emily Gravett

Years 5-8
Wolves in the Walls by Neil Gaiman
Varmints by Helen Ward
The Invention of Hugo Cabret by Brian Selznick
Archie's War by Marcia Williams
Flotsam by David Wiesner
Leon and the Place Between by Grahame Baker-Smith

The carers and children were encouraged to email any questions and work completed. Mid-way through the project a hub meeting was organised for carers to meet and share progress and hopefully gain more ideas from the other participants. During the summer holiday consultant visits to the home or a library nearby were proposed.

Phase 3 Evaluation of impact

A questionnaire (Figure 6.3) was sent to the carers and children with the intention of evaluating the project from both perspectives. Questions were designed to ascertain which activities they had engaged in as well as likes, dislikes and comments on the resources. This was a pilot literacy project carried out in very new terrain. The children had been identified as a vulnerable group through the complex and individual circumstances that had resulted in them being placed in care, thus it was necessary to adopt a flexible approach to the support offered and for all adult parties to work sensitively with the children. The local authority's evaluation therefore proposed that the carers' responses were also relevant and would be helpful when revising the project for a new group of children.

Please return the following questionnaire by **Friday 16th September**

Name: _____

What has been enjoyed the most? (This could be a specific book, an activity, or one of the resources - the camera, photo album, Photo Story etc.)

_____

What did the child do?

_____

_____

_____

_____

What have you found out about what the child enjoys and dislikes from doing some of the activities?

Likes: _____

Dislikes: _____

Please ask the child to write a comment below:

Is there anything else that you would like to share with us about the project?

_____

_____

Figure 6. 3 Questionnaire sent to carers and children

Celebration event

The children's efforts were celebrated at the annual achievement event in Rufford Abbey Country Park. This was a high profile affair with approximately 200 children and carers from across the county attending and presentations given by councillors and key figures in the Children's Social Care and Education Standards and Inclusion divisions for the local authority. The event provided a platform to showcase the children's work on a stall and for consultants to present an outline of the project. Picturebooks were also shown which engaged the audience and encouraged some children to meet with the consultants later in the morning and express an interest in getting involved if another project was planned (Figure 6.4).

Figure 6.4 Stall providing information on the multimodal project and showcasing some of the children's work

Reflection and evaluation

Target group

The group size of twelve children was felt to be manageable and worked well with a good spread over KS1, 2 and into KS3 (Reception to year 7). This size meant that the consultants could include potentially up to thirty six adult participants for twelve children. However, for future projects it was agreed that it could be beneficial to cluster children in three to four schools in order to offer more concentrated support that could still address individual issues.

The ideal target group for this project would be reluctant readers who would benefit most from a multimodal approach to literacy. Stimulating, multi-layered texts that could be explored as they were read brought the texts alive for many of the children as they discussed both the printed text and the images.

Responses indicated that the children appeared to learn how to use Photo Story very quickly and enjoyed employing the different editing techniques to add further meanings. Interestingly, several began by taking pictures of the picture books and then recreated their own stories by inserting text. Others used this approach to highlight pages that they enjoyed and provided book reviews.

The carers' response

The training day which launched the project was positively received. Participants welcomed resources and appeared genuinely interested and committed to using this approach. However, further into the project, it was recognised that these families have complex lives; all of the carers explained that at times there had been more pressing issues for the young people, this in turn made follow-up meetings difficult to plan. Future projects will fully explain all expectations at the launch and ask participants to commit to dates at the very start of the project.

The consultants maintained contact with the carers who generally responded positively to emails and phone calls. Two carers sent Photo Story texts via email. However, none of the families took up offers from the consultants to make home visits, meet at local libraries or at the local authority venues to support the progress of project work. Those visits made to individual schools were felt to be valuable to driving the approach and maintaining links. One carer commented on how impressed she was with the talking albums and said that she intended to purchase them for the other three children in her care who attended another school. Similar comments and observations have now been considered and future projects will include scheduled follow up visits to schools to meet with children, carers and school lead and, when possible, will try to involve families who have more than one LAC in the family to encourage peer support.

Handwritten account

Table reservation card collected

Leaflet on how to look after her pet mouse given as a birthday present

Word-processed account of her day and picture of the children holding their new mouse

Figure 6.5 Eight year old girl's record of her birthday with her twin brother

An unexpected but very positive outcome was that many of the carers made a connection with another project that they were involved in; the resources seemed to work well alongside the ongoing 'Life Stories' records initiated by the children's social workers. Most of the families adopted the scrapbook idea presented in Marcia Williams' *Archie's War* picture book which was used as a model or prompt alongside the talking photo albums. The outcomes became either recounts of family outings and events or report style texts illustrating family members. The texts created were direct examples of the children responding to a multi-layered picturebook: taking pictures, writing captions, recording their narrations and arranging the information in purposeful ways to create meanings. Figures 6.5 and 6.6 show extracts from an eight year-old girl's talking photo album.

Report style writing on christening and confirmation events

Certificate

Envelope or certificate

Cards

Figure 6.6 Collection of texts to be entered in a talking photo album

The children's responses

The children evaluated the project positively and seemed to particularly enjoy using their digital cameras and uploading the pictures for Photo Story creations. They worked creatively with this process and were able to incorporate images from the picture books to create their own texts.

I thoroughly enjoyed the Photo Story and I got to use my imagination. 11 year-old girl

It was fantastic! 7 year-old girl

I really enjoyed it. 7 year-old boy

We enjoyed using the cameras. 8 and 10 year-olds

I have enjoyed the books… the pictures give me new ideas. 10 year-old girl

I take the camera with me everywhere. Look I will show you what I have been doing… do you want to see? I showed my class today too! 10 year-old girl

School support

A valuable opportunity at the launch of this project was to have both carer and a member of school staff together. This was felt to be important because it provided a time to share information and observations on the child (see Figure 6.2 for an example of information gathered). Activities that encouraged such discussions also established that in their everyday lives children adopt many roles and have many identities in the home and school domains. It was recognised that some of these roles are evident in their 'real life' routines and others in their fantasy play. The latter was recognised as often linked to popular culture and the group highlighted the 'funds of knowledge' (Moll *et al.*, 1992) that children can bring to a literacy activity based on their experiences of media narratives. This discussion also included acknowledgement of young people's skills in working with technology, for example, an eleven year-old boy's school mentor spoke about how motivated he was when playing a word making activity on his iPhone each week during their meetings. The project proved particularly beneficial for this young person:

Normally a quiet young man, he became animated and confident as he read out the script he had worked on to go with his photographs. He laughed a lot and managed the inevitable problems in recording with patience and good humour. His reading of the script which he had prepared with help was clear and confident.

What I can say is that the project proved in its early stages to boost Kevin's confidence with books and writing and speaking. He has gone on to access reading support in the school and this we must take as a very positive outcome. (School mentor)

The willingness of the child's school to continue actively to support this work beyond the launch is of equal importance to the supportiveness of carers. Overall, it was felt that those children who also had the ongoing support and interest of their school benefited most from the project. It was concluded that with increased funding, headteachers would be more inclined to provide more class teacher time and support. In her evaluation, one carer highlighted that she had expected more support from the child's school. More positive responses had shown that schools recognise the potential of some of the resources such as Photo Story and were keen to develop this in school. It is hoped that in future projects, with added funding and more support from schools, other children would also benefit from the multimodal activities.

Next steps

The revised programme of support (Figure 6.7) brings the project full circle and aims to embed learning and skills to support further participants. The pilot study ran for six months but it is now intended to run through a school year and view the project as a cycle. In light of the evaluations a stronger commitment from schools is requested and planned for in order to support the child and carer and to embrace good practice in literacy teaching.

	Phase 1
September	Opportunity for children to sign up for the project at the Nottinghamshire Looked After Children's Achievement Event.
October	Participants are identified - some factors considered such as schools previously participating in multimodal projects, clusters of LAC in a school and interest shown by the children and carers in participating.
November	Training day launching the project for the year. The timing allows for the project work and ideas to be themed on the upcoming Christmas holidays.
	Phase 2
1-3 weeks after the launch	Consultant follow-up visits in schools, during lunchtimes or at the end of the school day. The content of support includes ICT needs and to provide assistance with ideas to motivate and encourage.
End of January	Half-day meeting for carers and school staff. The invitation for this event provides information about further resources to be given on the day and the session is an opportunity to share outcomes so far, ideas, issues and solutions. Discussion of the next multimodal literacy project to be carried out in February half-term holiday.
Early March	School visits by consultant to collect February project work and explain and support work for a celebration event in June.
	Phase 3
June	After school celebration event with readers, carers and school staff. In celebrating the children's work, 'champions in schools' to be identified for the larger annual county September achievement event. Other carers invited and current carers possibly involved in supporting the next group. Carers, children, schools and LA representatives to evaluate the project.

Figure 6.7 Revised programme of support

On reflection it would be better if the school staff involved had responsibility for literacy. Multimodal approaches to literacy have been noted positively in Ofsted inspections of Nottinghamshire schools and this could be used with school leaders to ensure support for the work with LAC as training and development for school staff to use across school.

Conclusion

The model of support developed around the importance of sharing observations from home and school. This combination of support alongside stimulating resources and an increasing understanding about the design of a text motivated the children to build and share. A project like this emphasises the importance of listening to children and working with their interests; embracing the challenges of their complex and sometimes upsetting lives can provide so much more for the child's learning potential.

Notes

[1] The use of the term 'looked after child' (LAC) was introduced by the Children's Act 1989 which put forward that 'looked after' refers to both children subject to care orders made by the court and those who are voluntarily accommodated (Grimshaw and Huggins, 2010; DCSF, 2010). Nottinghamshire county council defines 'looked after' as meaning 'cared for by us'. Broadly speaking, children who fall into this category are young people who cannot live with their parents. Grimshaw and Huggins state that: 'There are around 60,000 looked after children in the UK at any one time, amounting to 5% of all children and young people.' (2010:38).

[2] The main ICT software used was a free download of Microsoft's Photo Story 3. In addition to this, the local authority funded a number of key resources for each child. These included a digital camera with memory card, memory stick, £10 voucher for film processing, a talking photo album (Figure 6.1) head-set with microphone and three picture books. It was stressed that these items would remain with the children even if they moved onto another carer or back to their biological family.

Reflections

- What provision does your school make for vulnerable groups of children?
- How might you use digital technologies to help raise children's self-esteem and achievement in literacy?

Somali Voices *Codadka Soomaalida*: bilingual storytelling project

Marcia Sinclair

Background

> *The presence of Somali in England dates back to the early nineteen century. Although the majority of them came to London in the 80's and 90's as refugees and asylum seekers. (Kahin, 2007:15)*

Narrowing the gap for disadvantaged and vulnerable pupils is a national priority for local authorities and schools, with a focus on children on free school meals. London data shows an increasingly high number of Somali pupils living in north and west London (Figure 7.1); on average nearly 80% of these pupils are entitled to free school meals and they are identified as one of the lowest achieving groups. Recent arrivals include Somali families who have previously lived in the Netherlands, Germany, Sweden or Norway before arriving in the UK. They usually come to join other family members and reunite with their communities. Somali pupils comprise one of the fastest growing black African groups in north and west London schools.

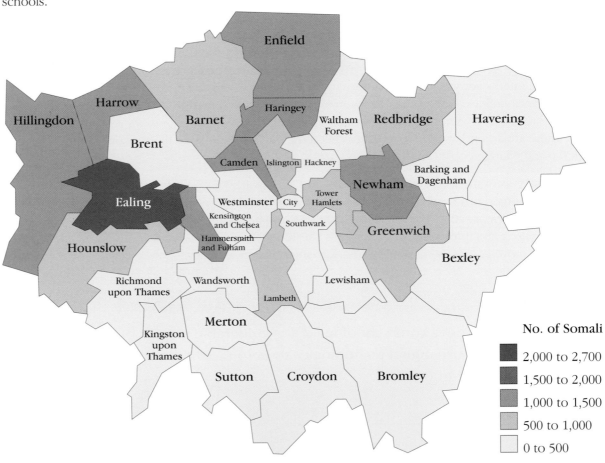

No. of Somali

- 2,000 to 2,700
- 1,500 to 2,000
- 1,000 to 1,500
- 500 to 1,000
- 0 to 500

Figure 7.1 Numbers of Somali children in London maintained schools, 2009

In Enfield, Somali pupils make up 4% of the pupil population and they are one of the fastest growing black African groups in Enfield. Somali is the second (3%) of the top five languages spoken by Enfield school pupils. Nationally Somali pupils' achievement is a concern. However, over the last three years Somali pupils in Enfield have made good progress although they remain one of the lowest attaining groups as evidenced by the 2009 ethnic data report (London borough of Enfield, 2009).

The three schools that participated in this project are on the eastern side of the borough in an area of high socio-economic deprivation. In this area there are third generation and newly arrived Somali families. Some of the families experience many problems which need additional support, including high levels of unemployment, large numbers of people in poor health, a higher than average percentage of lone parents, many households with low incomes and few opportunities for families to improve their quality of life. In addition, the families are concerned that many young people leave school with no qualifications. As part of a Black children's achievement programme in the London borough of Enfield, this project aimed to identify key strategies that would support the achievement of Somali pupils and identify the main barriers to educational success.

The project: Somali Voices

This community project was developed in response to requests from Somali parents who wanted to help their children be more successful in school. Children, teachers, parents, an outreach worker and librarians were involved in the project. We conducted a series of parents' interviews and learning conversations with pupils across key stage one and two in three schools, which were part of the Black children's achievement programme. The discussions established that:

- Somali parents and the Somali community place a high value on education
- parents and pupils have many hopes and aspirations for the future
- parents would like to support their children but may not know how because of a lack of knowledge of English school system
- there were few positive role models identified in the Somali community
- parents believed that feeling safe was essential to their children's success
- parents and pupils felt that Somali culture is often invisible in schools
- many parents said that they would like to see more opportunities to celebrate their presence and their culture in schools
- children born in the UK or who have been exposed to English for a considerable time often become less able to communicate with their parents in Somali which leads to a breakdown in communication
- it is important not assume that all children will be familiar with their family's country of origin.

During the discussions Somali parents outlined what they felt were the barriers to helping their children. These included their lack of confidence in English language skills and a lack of understanding of the British education system and the curriculum. From the above quotations, it was obvious that there was a great need for culturally relevant literature about and from Somalia in order to raise Somali pupils' and parents' self-esteem and to enhance their learning of English language and literacy.

In planning the project we listened to and tried to accommodate the differing views of Somali parents who were generous with their time. They spoke passionately about their country, their hopes for its future and the future for their children and community in Enfield. From the parents' meetings held in schools and libraries we established the following aims for the project:

- to promote self-esteem among Somali pupils in Enfield through providing a positive experience for the Somali community to enable them to contribute something of their special heritage to schools, classrooms, libraries and museums
- to use bilingual texts to promote literacy in both English and Somali
- to develop a resource bank of Somali stories, artefacts and information and to use it to help bridge the communication gap between schools, families and communities in Enfield.

The Somali Voices project took the form of a community of enquiry, a discussion method aimed at helping children and parents develop a variety of important communicational skills traditionally overlooked throughout their school career. The work was founded on a desire to allow children actively to engage with storytelling in a manner perhaps new to them - through a structured process encouraging creative activities and critical thought through discussion, talking partner activities, role play and drama. We planned to explore learning and teaching approaches which would maximize the achievement of Somali children and provide conditions for

Some of our children don't enjoy reading. We are concerned that they can get to Year 6 and still not be fluent competent readers. How can we get our children to enjoy reading books? If they leave school without reading well they will always be behind. We have a proverb in Somalia - Ignorance is like an illness...
Somali Parent

We need to show people what Somali culture is all about. When I go to schools, classrooms, libraries, museums, etc., I see things from all over the world but I don't see anything about Somalia.
Parent from Rayham primary school

When I go to the libraries (school and public) there are lots of traditional stories from other cultures and some are translated into different languages, including Somali. Why are there no traditional Somali folktales translated into English?
Parent from Hazelbury infant school

learning which value diversity and build and promote self-confidence. We particularly wanted to challenge racism and promote race equality and racial harmony through the curriculum and to develop effective partnership with parents, carers, families and communities.

Starting with stories

The project employed a storyteller and a bilingual Somali librarian to provide the children with the opportunity to develop their natural intelligences - logical, emotional and social - in a supportive peer-focused environment but also to develop their cultural identity through stories (Figure 7.2).

Figure 7.2 Storyteller telling 'The Lion's Share' story in Somali at Hazelbury infants school

For as long as human society has existed, story has been the vessel for passing on knowledge, history and culture. Although the oral tradition is no longer our only form of communication, we still love to tell stories - though today we may do it through multimodal framework: through films, photographs, enactment, the written or the sung word. Despite the many ways in which we now enjoy stories, the role of story remains unchanged as does the enthusiasm for the oral tradition.

Research into the effects of storytelling on young children has shown it to be effective in enhancing communication skills and improving problem solving (Grainger, 1997). It is also an accessible and human form of performing art that provides a wonderful return to the basics of human communication in today's increasingly high-tech, multimedia and potentially alienating society.

Figure 7.3 The people ran out of the village - children's illustration from 'Omar and the Hyena'

Telling stories is central to so much of what we do in all cultures. Parents reminisced about their experience of stories in Somalia:

> *In traditional meetings there is always a poet or a storyteller who started and finished the meetings with a story. Telling traditional tales to adults and children has been handed down from one generation to another generation.*
> Parent from Prince of Wales primary school

> *I tell stories to my children. I heard the stories from my dad. My mum died when I was young and my dad brought us up. He had to be both a mother and a father to us. So he was the one who told us stories and those are the stories that I tell to my children. They love to hear them. They never get tired of then. Even after they have heard them a hundred times they still say to me 'Mum, will you tell us a story?'*
> Parent from Bush Hill Park primary school

Figure 7.4 Display of artefacts from Somalia from the Somali Parents Group

A multimodal approach

As stories originated in the spoken word and are often accompanied by actions and song, and modern stories are often seen on screen, it was important to make the learning as multimodal as possible. Pictures, artefacts and music were used alongside the telling (Figures 7.3 and 7.4). The activities included:

- hearing storytellers: primary school classes had the opportunity to go to the library for an hour-long session of stories and related activities (e.g. craft or music)
- story boarding using cameras
- PowerPoint™ presentations as electronic books
- literacy circles and talking partners
- telling and acting out stories to groups, to camera and as radio broadcasts
- making films
- storytelling with parents
- illustrating stories
- collecting and sharing parents' stories.

Figure 7.5 Storytelling session with parents at Prince of Wales primary school

The five popular stories collected from parents[1] came from a rich Somali oral tradition that has been passed down from generation to generation. Not only are the stories familiar to the Somali parents but they also reflect their cultural and geographical context, the characters, values, lifestyles, climate, landscape, plants, etc; their very survival is threatened by war and geographical displacement. It was hoped that this project, in some way, would help to preserve a small part of Somalia's legacy.

All participating schools and libraries agreed that the starting point was to establish a storytelling ethos. The schools invited parents to a meeting not only to introduce them to the project but also to develop their confidence to participate in personal storytelling and sharing childhood traditional stories. The libraries also organised storytelling sessions (Figure 7.5).

Figure 7.6 Year one children retelling a story in both in Somali and English

Through listening to parents sharing personal stories about their past and researching traditional tales, the children learned about themselves, their backgrounds, culture and identity. The parents told the stories and they were retold by the children in the classroom (Figure 7.6). Through the telling and sharing of parents' favourite tales in the classroom, the commonality of parents' and children's experiences was evident (Figure 7.7). The personal and traditional tales became a resource bank for retelling with the parents, teachers and children. Five traditional tales were collected, translated and recorded both in written text and orally and made available on a CDROM (Figure 7.8).

The children's sharing of personal and traditional tales encouraged the teachers in one school to have regular storytelling session from different cultures. The school invited other teachers, parents, learning consultants, a librarian and professional storytellers to tell stories. Further, a storytelling area was designed and decorated using materials from Somalia and artefacts collected from parents.

Figure 7.7 Children from Prince of Wales school working with a support worker on illustrations for the books

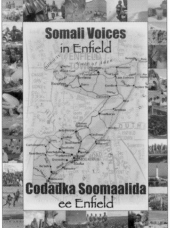

In one school the target was that all children in year five should become effective and engaging story tellers. The school identified that there were a few children who could learn stories off by heart but were not developed storytellers so they focused on developing strategies for story memory and used a professional storyteller and musician to help the children learn how to give a storytelling performance. At the end of the project they shared their stories with children in key stage one.

Figure 7.8 Cover of Somali Voices in Enfield Codadka Soomaalida ee Enfield

Reflections on the project

Many teachers in the project told us how the children loved hearing and working with the stories. Their storytelling, speaking, and listening skills improved and the children learned about the creative use of technology, but they also discovered a great deal about the natural world as well as about how stories work and how character is portrayed. They:

I was watching my daughter playing with her friend the other day. Suddenly she stopped and said to her: 'shall I tell you a story?' I listened to what she was going to say. She told one of our stories in English and Somali. It was our Somali story. She told it beautifully. I was so happy to hear her.
Somali parent from Hazelbury infants school

- explored attributes of animals portrayed in fables
- compared how animals behave in nature as contrasted with folklore
- developed a sense of the world's habitats described in folktales (jungles, deserts, mountains, meadows, etc)
- recognised patterns in folktales from different cultures about any animal (for example, bear stories, snake stories, fish stories, etc)
- expressed the interconnectedness, or ecology, of all things
- understood cause and effect in relationships expressed in folktales
- researched personal and traditional stories from parents
- developed story telling skills
- developed memory skills using a variety of strategies including storyboarding shaping and mapping.

More generally, in terms of learning, results indicated increases in thinking skills, for example, the ability to justify personal opinions, follow lines of thought to a logical conclusion and see connections between different areas of their knowledge and experience. The children's concentration, self-awareness, respect for others and their opinions and self-confidence also improved. In all three schools involved in the project, the Somali children's attainment improved and in one school the pupils are bucking the trend for achievement of Somali children both locally and nationally.

Teachers' assessments in all three schools showed the strongest increase in literacy and speaking and listening skills, suggesting that changes were occurring at a deep level within the individuals and giving credence to the claim that multimodal participation and talking to learn can help build literacy and cultural competency.

Conclusion

The Somali Voices project created positive awareness of heritage and identity, recognised and celebrated cultural and ethnic diversity. With its proactive partnership with parents, carers and the wider community, the project modelled partnership working with schools, parents, libraries, community groups and other agencies. Its success adds to already substantial evidence that storytelling, working with parents and focusing on talking to learn are appropriate and effective ways to move towards the educational goal of providing opportunities for the development of every child's full potential.

Notes

[1] The collection of stories *Somali Voices in Enfield/Codadka Soomaalida* has been published by Enfield Council.

Acknowledgements

Support and advice provided during the project:

Pauline Lyseight-Jones, regional adviser, National Strategies
Enfield primary literacy team
Enfield primary Ethnic Minority Achievement team
Dawn Kandetore, learning consultant, Delta City Learning Centre
Rachel Green, Enfield school improvement administrator (EMA).

Our greatest debt is to the, pupils, parents, headteachers, deputy headteachers, assistant headteachers, teachers and administrators of:

Raynham primary school: Marva Rollins, headteacher; Jan Humphries, administrator; Ann Heath, deputy headteacher.
Prince of Wales primary school: Carmel Moore, headteacher, and Julia Clarke, deputy headteacher; Yasmin Kapadia, EMA coordinator; Ms Hibat Samater, parent support worker.
Hazelbury infant school: Laurel Barber and Leslie Rose, deputy headteachers, Melanie Scull and Clyde Brennan, assistant head teachers; Shamsa Adan and Maryan Jimale, parent support workers.

Thanks also to:

Bush Hill Park primary school, Churchfield primary school, Fleecefield primary school
Claire Dalkin, Sumita Choudhury, and Hussein Hur of Enfield library service
Jan Metcalfe of Enfield museum service
Richard Neville: Stories in the Street
Hasan Adan: Enfield parents and children support in school
Kaltun Abdillahi: the Samafal Somali Women's Association.

Reflections

- How might you find out about parents' hopes and aspirations for their children's education?
- How do you ensure that children's cultures are visible in your school?
- What role does your school play in the community?
- Consider your work with parents and carers and other organisations (libraries, museums, etc).
- How might these links be developed to impact on the children's learning.

References

58

Anderson, J. and Chung, Y-C. (2010) Community languages, the arts and transformative pedagogy, in *Race Equality Teaching* 28(3) pp 16-20.

Bearne, E. with Bazalgette, C. (2010) *Beyond words: Developing children's response to multimodal texts*. Leicester: United Kingdom Literacy Association.

Black, P., Harrison, C., Lee, C., Marshall, B. and Wiliam, D. (2002) *Working Inside The Black Box: Assessment for Learning in the Classroom*. London: Department of Education and Professional Studies, King's College London.

Blatchford, P. (2003) *The Class Size Debate: is small better?* Buckingham: Open University Press.

Bourdieu, P. (1986) The forms of capital, in J. Richardson (Ed.) *Handbook of Theory and Research for the Sociology of Education*. New York: Greenwood pp 241-258.

Comber, B. (2001) Critical literacies and local action: teacher knowledge and a 'new' research agenda. In B. Comber and A. Simpson (Eds) *Negotiating critical literacies in classrooms*. New Jersey: Lawrence Erlbaum.

Comber, B. (2007) Assembling dynamic repertoires of literate practices: teaching that makes a difference, in E. Bearne and J. Marsh (Eds) *Literacy and Social Inclusion: Closing the Gap*. Stoke on Trent: Trentham Books.

Comber, B. and Kamler, B. (2004) Getting Out Of Deficit: pedagogies of reconnection. *Teaching Education* 15 (3) pp 293-310.

Cremin, T., Mottram, M., Collins, F., Powell, S., and Drury, R. (2011) *Building Communities: Researching Literacy Lives 2009-10 Executive Summary*. Leicester: United Kingdom Literacy Association. http://www.ukla.org/research/research_projects_in_progress/_uklaou_building_communities researching_literacy_lives_/
Accessed February 20th, 2012.

Demie, F. McLean, C. Lewis, K. (2008) *Raising Achievement in Somali Pupils: good practice in London schools*. London Borough of Lambeth: Lambeth Research and Statistics Unit.

Department for Culture Media and Sport (2010) *Promoting the Educational Achievement of Looked After Children: Statutory Guidance for Local Authorities*. Nottingham: DCSF Publications.

Department for Education (2011) *The Framework for the National Curriculum: A report by the Expert Panel for the National Curriculum review*. London: Department for Education. http://www.education.gov.uk/schools/teachingandlearning/curriculum/nationalcurriculum
Accessed February 20th, 2012.

Dweck, C. (1989) Motivation, in A. Lesgold and R. Glaser *Foundations for a Psychology of Education*. Hillsdale, NJ: Erlbaum.

Ealing School Improvement Team: EMA Team (2009) *Raising the Achievement of Somali Pupils in Ealing: Case studies of good practice*. London Borough of Ealing.

Garcia, O. (2009) Bilingual Education in the 21st Century: A global perspective, in *Race Equality Teaching*. 28(3) pp 8-14.

Gonzalez, N., Moll, L. and Amanti, C. (2005) *Funds of Knowledge: Theorizing practice in households, communities and classrooms*. London: Lawrence Erlbaum.

Grainger, T. (1997) *Traditional Storytelling in the Primary Classroom*. Leamington Spa: Scholastic.

Grimshaw, C. and Huggins, M. (editors) (2010) *Designated Teacher Guidebook: the definitive guide to being an effective designated teacher*. London: Care Matters Partnership Ltd.

Kahin, M.H. (1997) *Educating Somali Children in Britain*. Stoke on Trent: Trentham Books.